Presenting
THAILAND
A Journey through the Kingdom

Presenting
THAILAND
A Journey through the Kingdom

TEXT BY JOHN HOSKIN
PHOTOGRAPY BY MARK STANDEN

✳ ASIA BOOKS

✳ ASIA BOOKS

Published and Distributed by
ASIA BOOKS CO., LTD
NO# 65/66, 65/70, 7TH FLOOR,
CHAMNAN PHENJATI BUSINESS CENTER
RAMA 9 ROAD, HUAYKWANG,
BANGKOK 10320 THAILAND
Tel: (66 2) 715-9000
Fax: (66 2) 715-9197
E-mail: information@asiabooks.com
www.asiabooks.com

10 9 8 7 6 5 4 3 2 1

ISBN 978-1-906780-37-1

Edited, designed and typeset by Stonecastle Graphics
Cartography by William Smuts

Printed and bound in Singapore by Tien Wah Press (Pte) Ltd.

All photographs © **Mark Standen**, with the exception of the following.
© **Leon Schadeberg**: 35(r), 50(a), 50(b), 51(l), 51(r).
© **Shutterstock.com**: Prasit Chansareekorn 62(b); Kushch Dmitry 38(a);
gh19 53(b); MOL endpapers; Luciano Mortula 70(a); phloen 53(ar);
Tiggy Gallery! 53(al).

Page 1: Local fishing boats in the far southern province of Satun are caught in the glow of the late afternoon sun.

Pages 2 and 3: Evening view of the Buddha statue and spires of twin *chedis* at Wat Phra That Doi Kong Mu, Mae Hong Son.

Right: A three-wheeled tuk tuk passes the ornate entrance to Wat Phra That Phanom in the northeastern province of Nakhon Phanom.

Contents

Opposite above left: Like a sea of white, mist swirls around the base of the cliffs at Phu Chee Fah, Chiang Rai province.

Above left: Rice cultivation in the fertile valleys of the north, an area historically known as Lanna, meaning 'a million rice fields'.

Left: Wat Chiang Man is believed to be Chiang Mai's oldest temple, its site dating back to the late 13th century.

Opposite below left: Statues of mythical giants, *yaksha*, guard against evil spirits at the entrance to Wat Phra Kaeo in Bangkok.

Introduction

"It is now a cliché to style Thailand the 'Land of Smiles', but the fact that the phrase is overused makes it no less true."

My first impression of Thailand was one of wonder amid chaos. Stuck in impossible traffic, with jumbled lines of cars, trucks, buses, motorbikes and tuk-tuks, Bangkok's iconic three-wheeled taxis, all jockeying for position to gain an extra yard seemed an exercise in sheer futility. Then, finally arrived at my destination, the Temple of the Emerald Buddha, with its sweeping orange and green tiered roofs and gilded spires, was so beguiling in its exotic design and aura of serenity as to dispel utterly any previous sense of impending chaos.

That was 30 years ago and today everything and nothing has changed. With expressways, flyovers and ring roads, as well as two mass transit systems, getting around Bangkok is no longer quite the madness it once was, while the Temple of the Emerald Buddha remains as glorious as ever in its architectural wonder and power to inspire awe.

Similarly, attractions around the country as diverse as the forested hills of the north and the white-sand beaches of the south continue to exert an irresistible magnetism, as witnessed by visitor arrivals that have grown from a few hundred thousands in the 1970s to what is now around 15 million annually.

Indeed, tourism, along with highly successful efforts to expand exports and to attract foreign investment that occurred in the 1980s and 1990s, powered the Thai economy, bringing unprecedented prosperity. This was most visible in a massive construction boom which has altered the face of Bangkok, as well as numerous cities and resorts around the country. Increased prosperity has also brought social change, particularly the emergence of an urban middle class that has taken an increasing stake in the nation's development.

And yet in spite of the economic and social change powered by modernization and westernization, Thailand retains a sense of exoticism, a quality of being elsewhere, that is scarcely matched by any other country. A rich history and a rare variety of landscapes are a big part of the allure, though the wealth of cultural and natural attractions, real though they are, do not alone account for the Kingdom's exotic appeal. More than anything else Thailand

THE WAI

Every culture has its own custom of greeting, a characteristic way of introducing oneself and paying one's respects to others; for the Thais it is the *wai*. This is performed by raising the hands, palms together, to a position lightly touching the body somewhere between chest and forehead. The head is slightly bent when *wai*-ing, and the whole movement should be performed slowly and gracefully. Simple though it appears, the *wai* has its finer points.

For example, the higher the hands are raised, the greater the respect being shown. Also it is correct protocol for a younger person, or someone of junior status, to be the first to *wai* before the senior returns the gesture. A greeting, a farewell, a show of respect or of thanks, the *wai* is an essential courtesy and a defining social custom.

possesses a curious and continuing ability to surprise, which springs from two quintessential characteristics: a quality of 'Thai-ness' and an easy accommodation of the paradoxical.

Pervading and defining the culture is a certain style, a gentle refinement and a way of doings things that is inimitably Thai and is found nowhere else. This is clearly manifest in the arts, in the stylized moves of Thai classical dance, for example, or in the smooth flowing lines of traditional Buddha sculptures. In daily life, it is the gracious *wai* greeting that most readily exemplifies an inescapable grace and charm.

Less obvious is the Thainess inherent in the culture's remarkable ability to adopt and adapt. Throughout their history the Thais have absorbed alien influences and transformed them into something singularly their own. Take food; the Thai culinary art draws on Indian, Burmese, Chinese and Malay influences, not to mention the ubiquitous chilli that was introduced to the country by the Portuguese, but the result is so appealing and so distinct as to make it one of the world's great national cuisines, today popularized in restaurants around the world.

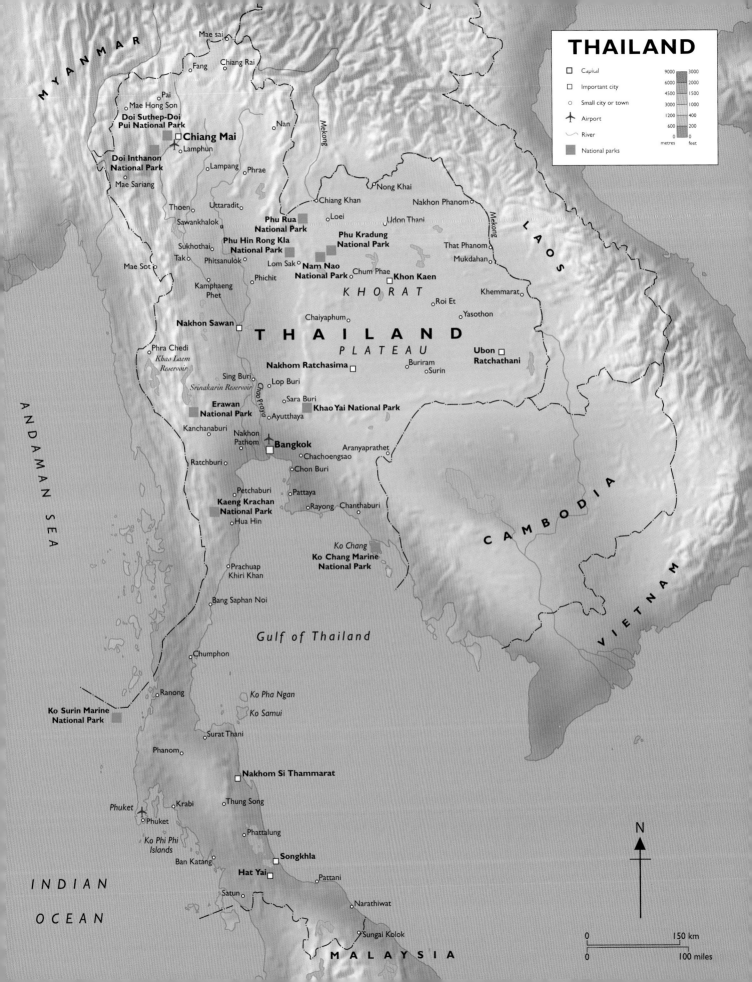

MYANMAR

Mae sai
Chiang Rai
Fang
Pai
Mae Hong Son
Doi Suthep-Doi
Pui National Park
Chiang Mai
Lamphun
Doi Inthanon
National Park
Mae Sariang
Nan
Lampang
Phrae

MEKONG

Nong Khai
Chiang Khan
Nakhon Phanom
Loei
Udon Thani
Phu Rua
National Park
That Phanom
Mukdahan

LAOS

Thoen
Uttaradit
Sawankhalok
Phu Hin Rong Kla
National Park
Phu Kradung
National Park
Sukhothai
Tak
Phitsanulok
Lom Sak
Nam Nao
National Park
Chum Phae
Khon Kaen
Mae Sot
Phichit
KHORAT
Kamphaeng
Phet
Khemmarat
Chaiyaphum
Roi Et
Yasothon
Nakhon Sawan
THAILAND
PLATEAU
Ubon
Ratchathani
Phra Chedi
Khao Laem
Reservoir
Sing Buri
Nakhom Ratchasima
Buriram
Surin
Srinakarin Reservoir
Lop Buri
CHAO PHRAYA
Erawan
National Park
Sara Buri
Khao Yai National Park
Ayutthaya
Kanchanaburi
Nakhon
Pathom
Bangkok
Aranyaprathet
Chachoengsao
Ratchburi
Chon Buri
Petchaburi
Pattaya
Kaeng Krachan
National Park
Rayong
Chanthaburi
Hua Hin

CAMBODIA

ANDAMAN SEA

Prachuap
Khiri Khan
Ko Chang
Ko Chang Marine
National Park
Bang Saphan Noi

VIETNAM

Gulf of Thailand

Chumphon

Ranong
Ko Pha Ngan
Ko Samui
Ko Surin Marine
National Park
Surat Thani
Phanom
Nakhom Si Thammarat
Phuket
Krabi
Thung Song
Phuket
Phattalung
Ko Phi Phi
Islands
Songkhla
Ban Katang
Hat Yai
Pattani
Satun
Narathiwat
INDIAN
OCEAN
Sungai Kolok

MALAYSIA

0   150 km
0   100 miles

Paralleling Thainess as a source of surprise are the paradoxes in which the Kingdom abounds. Respect for the old, love of the new; devotion to the sacred, delight in the profane; pride in Oriental splendour, enthusiasm for Western glitter – these and other seeming contradictions sit so comfortably with the Thais that they really do appear to have the best of both worlds. The sensation is contagious and casts a profound spell.

A pronounced sense of Thainess, a juggling of the paradoxical, a history of proud independence, all the intriguing complexities of Thai culture are indelibly coloured by one thing – fun. Thailand is above all else about enjoying yourself, and the Thais have a word for it, *sanuk*. It is almost impossible to translate but it means everything that is pleasurable, that promises a good time.

Deeply ingrained, *sanuk* does not just imply the fun of recreation, or a night out; it's an approach to life in general and relates to all things at all times. Going for a stroll, meeting friends, shopping, eating, are all sources of *sanuk*. Of course, the Thais do see a serious side to life; the point is not to dwell on it unduly when there is so much else to enjoy.

Frequently paradoxical, always surprising ('amazing', as the Tourism Authority's slogan has it), Thailand is possessed of a timelessness even as it marches forward with the times – but to a tune of its own, naturally.

THE THAI SMILE

It is now a cliché to style Thailand the 'Land of Smiles', but the fact that the phrase is overused makes it no less true. The Thais do smile easily and genuinely out of pleasure and as an expression of their innate sense of hospitality.

The social mores of the Thais are complex and, aside from being a welcoming expression, the smile stems in part from the convention that one should not cause another to lose face, and the smile is the best possible face to present to the world.

Above: Much of Thailand remains rural and farmers working in the rice fields present an archetypal image.

Opposite: The golden Phra Si Rattana Chedi towers over the temple complex of Bangkok's Wat Phra Kaeo.

Left: Buddhist monks on their morning alms round pass by an old wooden shop-house in Nathon, Ko Samui's main town.

Opposite: A blissful scene prevails as the sun sets over Hat Nopparat, one of Krabi's most pristine and beautiful beaches.

Below: Almost a still life study of northern Thai style, a man with trishaw and traditional water jars pictured in Lamphun.

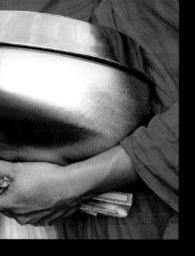

Chapter One

Thailand in Outline

The Land of Smiles

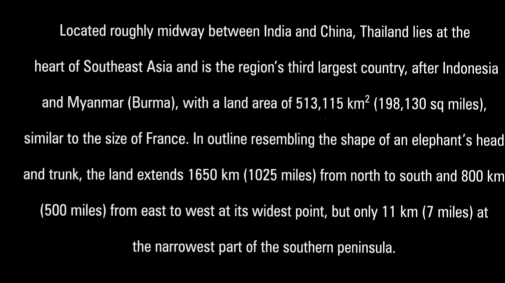

Located roughly midway between India and China, Thailand lies at the

heart of Southeast Asia and is the region's third largest country, after Indonesia

and Myanmar (Burma), with a land area of 513,115 km^2 (198,130 sq miles),

similar to the size of France. In outline resembling the shape of an elephant's head

and trunk, the land extends 1650 km (1025 miles) from north to south and 800 km

(500 miles) from east to west at its widest point, but only 11 km (7 miles) at

the narrowest part of the southern peninsula.

Opposite above left: Mythical *garudas* holding *naga* snakes surround
the base of the main shrine at Bangkok's Wat Phra Kaeo.

Above left: Monks clutch traditional alms bowls to receive food offerings from
the lay community on morning rounds.

Opposite left: A deckchair seller greets customers with a broad smile
on the beach at Hua Hin.

Left: Monkeys with a head for heights are skilled in the task of collecting
the coconut harvest on Ko Samui.

Thailand in Outline

"Climatically, Thailand is a tropical monsoon country where heat and high humidity are the predominant features."

The nation's borders are defined by Myanmar to the west and northwest, Laos to the northeast, Cambodia to the east and Malaysia to the south, while flanking the peninsula are the Andaman Sea on the west coast and the Gulf of Thailand on the east, giving a total coastline of 3219 km (2000 miles).

A land of contrasts, Thailand divides into four main regions: the north, which is primarily an area of mountains and steep river valleys and occupies about one-quarter of the nation's area; the northeast, a semi-arid plateau comprising roughly one-third of the country; the fertile Central Plains, traditionally 'the rice bowl of the nation' and watered by the Chao Phraya River, the country's principal waterway; and the south, comprising the long narrow stretch of peninsula Thailand.

Climatically, Thailand is a tropical monsoon country where heat and high humidity are the predominant features, although there are three seasons: hot-dry from February to May, when the temperature in Bangkok averages 34.5 °C (94 °F); rainy from June to October; and cool from November to January, during which period Bangkok temperatures range from 32 to below 20 °C (90 to below 68 °F). There are however, some regional differences; the north and northeast, for example, experience greater extremes of temperature range. In the past, the character and cyclic nature of the seasons was unvarying, but in this age of global warming they have become less predictable.

MONSOON CYCLE

Wet rice cultivation has traditionally sustained Thai life, and the agricultural cycle is dictated by the annual alternation of the southwest and northeast monsoons. These winds bring, respectively, the rainy and the dry-cool seasons, and the cycle governs the agricultural calendar of wet rice cultivation, the staple crop.

The rice cycle begins with the coming of the rains, which soften the earth and allow for ploughing, a task that traditionally relied on the water buffalo although today the animal has in part been replaced by the mechanical plough, the 'iron buffalo'. The back-breaking work of transplanting bright green rice seedlings takes place during the rainy season, when the paddy fields are flooded, and is done entirely by hand. After this, farmers enjoy comparative ease as they wait for the crop to ripen.

Finally, the labour-intensive harvesting of the ripened golden stalks takes place in the middle of the cool season.

Opposite: Mist shrouds the jungle-clad mountains that form the border with Myanmar in Kaeng Krachan National Park, Prachuab Khiri Khan province.

Flora and Fauna

If seasonal changes seem marginal compared to those experienced in temperate climes, Thailand's flora and fauna are remarkably varied. Due to the shape of the country, with its exceptionally long north-south reach, habitats differ hugely, ranging from dry areas through to those with plentiful rainfall. Although the natural environment has been moulded by the hands of man, especially through farming and deforestation – the latter activity having reduced forest cover from some 70 per cent of the land in the late 1930s to between 15 and 20 per cent today – diversity remains. Moreover, the creation of national parks and conservation areas in all regions of the country over the last 50 years has done much to help preserve a rich, though fragile, natural heritage.

Travelling from the coast to the hills, habitats range from mangrove forest and wetlands, through tropical rainforest, mixed deciduous forest and dry deciduous woodlands to evergreen rainforest, hill evergreen rainforest and montane evergreen forest. Complementing forest diversity, other flora includes bamboo, some 12,000 species of flowering plants, of which over a thousand species of orchid are the most celebrated, and an incredible array of exotic fruits for which Thailand is renowned.

Although numbers are dwindling and there is a pressing need for greater conservation efforts, Thailand's fauna is as diverse as its flora. Of indigenous mammals, around 300 species are found in the country, mainly in national parks and conservation areas, and they include elephants, tigers, clouded leopards, gaur, sambar deer, basking deer, tapir, gibbons and macaques. In terms of reptiles and amphibians Thailand can boast 313 and 107 species respectively, among which are several varieties of snakes, including the king cobra, and four species of sea turtles. In the particularly rich and

colourful underwater world are found more than 400 species of fish and some 250 species of hard corals.

It is in the richness of its bird life, however, that Thailand is truly amazing, with well over 1000 species recorded, both resident and migratory, and bird-watching has become a major attraction in recent years. Like other fauna, bird populations are largely demarcated by the country's long north-south axis. Among forest avifauna there are 12 species of hornbill, the largest being the great hornbill, while on the coastal and inland waterways of the southern peninsula waterfowl remain significant (although numbers have declined in recent years) and they include the Asian openbill stork, cormorants, egrets and night-herons.

Above: Mangroves, seen here near Khao Sam Roi Yot National Park, are a vital, yet threatened, part of the coastal ecosystem.

Opposite: A tranquil view of the table-top plateau at Phu Kradung National Park, Loei province, one of Thailand's most scenic spots.

Left: A family of dusky langurs photographed in the forest of Kaeng Krachan National Park, Prachuab Khiri Khan province.

Opposite above left: Various species of hornbills, including this pied hornbill, are notable members of Thailand's rich avian population.

Opposite above right: Egrets and other waterfowl are common on the coastal and inland waterways of the southern peninsula.

Opposite below: Bamboo is prolific and more species grow in Thailand than in any other country apart from China.

Below: The inland sea of Thale Noi, in Phattalung province, is maintained as a wildlife preserve, noted for both its flora and birdlife.

The Thai Elephant

A national icon, the elephant has enjoyed an exalted status throughout Thailand's history and played significant roles in the Kingdom's social, economic and cultural development

The most colourful and most dramatic historical part played by the elephant was that of a battle animal, a sort of forerunner of the tank. Typically the mount of kings – and queens – elephants regaled in battle harnesses, with their warrior riders mounted in a lightweight howdah and armed with spears and swords, would charge into the enemy and break up their ranks.

Also with regal associations are the rare white, or albino, elephants which are the exclusive property of the King and are traditionally believed to augur well for the success of the reign. These animals are highly revered and expensively maintained – a possible derivation of the term 'a white elephant', meaning something unproductive yet costly.

In representational form the elephant has been depicted in countless murals and illustrated manuscripts; it was once engraved on Thai coins, and from 1819 to 1917 the national flag pictured a white elephant on a red background. In Buddhist legend, too, the animal looms large. For example, one of the Jataka tales relates how the Buddha in a former life was born as a white elephant with six tusks emitting magical rays. Popular myths are also common and the animal is generally regarded as a symbol of good fortune, it being especially lucky, so they say, to pass beneath the belly of an elephant.

Yet for all the myths, legends and regal standing, it is as a humble work animal that the elephant has made its greatest mark. In the late 19th and early 20th centuries when teak logging was a major industry in the forests of northern Thailand, trained elephants provided the essential means of traversing difficult terrain and

extracting logs, hauling, pushing and stacking the heavy timber. Although teak logging has been banned since 1989, elephant training camps remain where visitors can watch demonstrations of the animal's refined forestry skills.

Regrettably, the number of elephants in Thailand has declined alarmingly over the last few decades, and it is estimated that the population of domestic elephants is now around 2500, compared to 100,000 a century ago.

Above left: Brick and stucco elephant buttresses are characteristic features of ancient temple architecture, especially that of the Sukhothai era.

Above and opposite: Whether displaying logging skills at conservation centres or trekking in the hills, the elephant still has a useful role to play.

People

Human habitation of the land now defined by Thailand, known as Siam until 1939, dates back at least 10,000 years, and linguistic studies, along with archaeological finds, at one time suggested that the Mekong River valley and the Khorat Plateau, an area that covers large parts of present-day Thailand, Laos and Cambodia, was a contender for the title 'cradle of civilization', where, on the path of migrations out of southern China, *Homo sapiens* first evolved as agriculturalists and metal workers.

Archaeological discoveries at Ban Chiang in northeast Thailand did at first seem to indicate that the site was a core area for the working of bronze in the 4th millennium BC. However, the finds were subsequently more accurately dated to between 2500 BC and 2000 BC. This is later than the first appearance of bronze and copper in the Middle East, but it does show that Thailand did have a true Bronze Age civilization. Moreover, there is evidence of rice cultivation as early as 3000 BC.

Whether the inhabitants of Ban Chiang were Tai, that is members of the Tai ethnic group to which the Thai, citizens of Thailand, largely belong, is less certain. The favoured theory, although by no means uncontested, is that the Tai who came to populate what is now Thailand originated in southern China, where various small tribal states united to form the kingdom of Nan Chao, in what is now China's Yunnan province. Nan Chao fell to the Mongol army of Kublai Khan in 1253, causing a mass exodus south. However, it is likely the southern migration of the Tai had begun before this and was a protracted affair, slowly populating a land that had been occupied by earlier civilizations, in particular those of the Mon and Khmer. As the Tai moved into the area now defined by Thailand's borders they gradually assumed dominance over these earlier civilizations, and became their cultural heirs.

The Thais of today are a product of this fusion and the overwhelming majority of the Kingdom's 67 million population speaks a dialect of Thai and shares a common culture. Four main subdivisions, however, are recognizable: the central Thais (the dominant group in terms of cultural and political hegemony) who speak the standard language; the Pak Isan Thais in the northeast, who are a mixture of Thai and Khmer; the Pak Thai Thais who inhabit the southern peninsula; and the northern Thais, a fusion between Thai incomers and Karen and Lawa hill-tribe peoples who were already settled in the region. All of the latter three groups speak Thai with their own distinct dialect.

Above left and right: Children from Muslim fishing communities seen in, respectively, Krabi and Songkhla. Although the vast majority of the population is Buddhist, Muslims form the largest religious minority, concentrated mostly in the country's southernmost provinces.

Opposite: Khao Sam Roi Yot National Park presents a fascinating variety of habitats, from wetlands to craggy mountains.

WATER WORLD

Traditionally the Thais are an aquatic people, or perhaps that should be amphibious.

'The highways of Bangkok are not streets or roads, but the river and the canals. Boats are the universal means of conveyance and communication … The existence of the people of Bangkok may be called amphibious. The children pass much of their time in the water, paddling and diving and swimming, as if it were their native element.'

So wrote Queen Victoria's envoy to Thailand, Sir John Bowring, in the 1850s, thus reinforcing Bangkok's then reputation as the 'Venice of the East', a title the city could merit until well into the 20th century when gradually more and more canals were filled in to make paved roads.

Though it wasn't only Bangkok that was built around waterways; throughout history until the modern period Thai towns and villages were developed beside water courses, which provided irrigation for wet rice cultivation and served as transportation links.

This is perhaps hard to imagine because of the present-day dominance of the motor car, but Bangkok's famous Floating Market, a major tourist attraction where fresh produce is sold from small boats plying the canals, is a reminder of earlier times.

Among non-Tai peoples, the Chinese form by far the largest group, around 11 per cent of the total population. Chinese traders had long settled in the coastal towns of peninsula Thailand, but the most significant migration took place during the 19th and early 20th centuries, when Bangkok's Chinese population grew from around 230,000 to more than 790,000. It was at that time that the Kingdom began to develop international trade with the West and it was the Chinese, more experienced in commerce than the Thais, who worked as merchants and middlemen. Today, people with Chinese ancestry make up a sizeable part of most urban populations, although assimilation has been such that differences are scarcely discernible.

Migratory patterns in the past have also given rise to other minority groupings, mostly confined to specific areas. They include the Lao-speaking people inhabiting parts of northeast Thailand, Khmer in the border areas of northeast Thailand and Cambodia, Shan (or Thai Yai) in the north, Mons, particularly in the provinces surrounding Bangkok, and Malays in the far south.

Most colourful and distinct among minority groups are the hill tribes of northern Thailand, which comprise six main groups: Karen, Lawa, Akha, Hmong, Mien (Yao) and Lahu, which together make up a population of about 500,000. Apart from the Karen and Lawa, who inhabited the region prior to the arrival of the Thais, these tribal peoples are relative newcomers, who began to move into the area at the end of the 19th century. Living mostly outside mainstream society and preserving individual cultural identities, most visible in their distinctive traditional costumes, the hill tribes are semi-nomadic and dependent on subsistence agriculture.

Above: Stone statues of warriors brought from China stand guard at Wat Arun, Temple of Dawn, in Bangkok.

Above left: Minority groups of hill tribes inhabiting northern Thailand are distinguished by their traditional costumes.

Above: A wizened-faced trishaw driver smiles for the camera in the northeastern city of Nakhon Ratchasima .

Above right: Women of the Padaung tribal minority found near Mae Hong Son are distinguished by brass neck rings worn since childhood.

Right: A child sports the typical northern attire and floral adornment worn during the Songkran festival.

Opposite: Traditionally hatted, a vendor paddles her boat along the canals of the Floating Market, Bangkok.

INDIANIZATION

Much of the culture, customs and beliefs of Thailand and elsewhere in Southeast Asia have their roots in ancient Indian civilization, which impacted on the region in a process known as 'Indianization'.

Beginning in the 1st century AD and continuing over the next five centuries, Indian merchants and other travellers touched on the shores of Southeast Asia while following the sea trade routes to China. Some stayed, settled and mixed with the local populations who, in turn, assimilated or modified various ideas of art, architecture, government and religion learned from the new arrivals.

Above: Wat Phra Phai Luang is one of the most extensive and important of the temple ruins at Sukhothai.

Opposite: The Buddha image and chedi of Wat Mahathat are classic reminders of the glory that once was Sukhothai.

Historical Outline

Thailand's early history, up to the middle of the 1st millennium, constitutes a 'dark age' because of the absence of any written records, and it is only from the 6th century AD onwards that a pattern of independent states in what is now Thailand begins to emerge. The three most powerful of these developed formative civilizations that laid down the cultural and administrative foundations on which the Thai would later build.

The earliest of these pre-Thai civilizations was the Mon kingdom of Dvaravati, which held sway between the 6th and 11th centuries AD in what is now central Thailand. More strictly a collection of city states, Dvaravati was centred variously at U Tong, close to the later Thai capital of Ayutthaya, Lopburi and Nakhon Pathom, which lies just west of Bangkok, all of which were centres of Theravada Buddhism, the faith subsequently adopted by the Thais.

By the 11th and 12th centuries, the Mon dominance of central Thailand declined as the Khmer, whose civilization was centred on Angkor in present-day Cambodia, expanded their empire westward, as attested today by ancient Khmer ruins scattered widely throughout northeast Thailand, and found as far west as Kanchanaburi and south in Petchburi province.

The third principal kingdom of this pre-Thai period was that of Srivijaya, which was dominant in the southern peninsula from the 7th to the 13th century. It is thought that Srivijaya's power base was centred on Sumatra, in Indonesia, although both the southern Thai town of Nakhon Si Thammarat and Chaiya, in present-day Surat Thani province, are believed to have been important outposts. Mostly of Malay stock, the people of Srivijaya held at first to the Hindu faith and later embraced Mahayana Buddhism.

By the early decades of the 13th century, the power of the pre-Thai civilizations was on the wane, while Thais had become strong enough and numerous enough to form petty states. Around 1240, two Thai chieftains joined forces, rallied their people and, with a united front, succeeded in defeating the Khmer at Sukhothai on the northern edge of the Central Plains. Following the victory, one of the chieftains was crowned King Intratit, and the first Thai sovereign state was formed.

During the first two reigns – those of King Sri Intratit and his son, King Ban Muang (died c.1279) – nothing disturbed the peace of the young kingdom which remained small, scarcely extending beyond the capital city. It was in the reign of King Ramkhamhaeng (c.1279–1298) that Sukhothai experienced its golden age. Under this monarch's masterful leadership the kingdom expanded dramatically and exerted control, directly or indirectly, over much of the land now defined by Thailand's borders. At the same time, unity was consolidated by the adoption of Theravada Buddhism as the national religion.

As the undisputed power base of the new Thai nation, Sukhothai reigned supreme for only 140 years. In 1378 it became a vassal of the younger Thai kingdom of Ayutthaya and 60 years later was totally absorbed by it. Yet in that brief time Sukhothai established religious, cultural and political patterns that have continued to underpin the nation.

Ayutthaya, Sukhothai's successor, was founded in 1350 after, according to legend, Prince U Thong, later crowned King Ramathibodi, slew a dragon that had terrorized the land around the junction of the Chao Phraya, Lopburi and Pa Sak rivers. Establishing a new Thai kingdom, U Thong commenced the construction of an island city – Ayutthaya – that rose to become one of the largest and wealthiest capitals in Southeast Asia, remaining dominant for more than 400 years.

During the Ayutthaya period, control was exerted over the entire Central Plains and, from the late 16th century, over the southern peninsula. Substantial reforms were made in administration, law and the military, while the arts flourished, particularly Buddhist sculpture, royal and religious architecture, temple mural painting and dance drama.

Making it all possible was enormous wealth based on the abundant agricultural output of the surrounding plains, and on international trade, with European merchant ships able to navigate the Chao Phraya River right up to the city. Indeed, one of the defining features of the Ayutthaya period was its fostering of relations with the West. A treaty with Portugal was made in 1516 and was followed by similar trade agreements with the Dutch, in 1604, and the British in 1612.

International relations peaked during the reign of King Narai (ruled 1656–1688), with French Catholic missionaries arriving in 1662. These became an important force in Franco-Thai diplomacy, which led to Louis XIV of France sending two ambassadorial missions to Ayutthaya in 1685 and 1687. However, conservative elements at court were suspicious of foreign influence and staged a revolution in 1688 after which most foreigners were expelled from the country.

Throughout its history, Ayutthaya was embroiled in intermittent warfare with the Burmese. The city fell to this traditional enemy in 1569, but regained independence less than two decades later and reasserted its strength and glory during the ensuing reign of King Naresuan (ruled 1590–1605). In 1767, however, the Burmese attacked once more and after a 14-month siege succeeded in taking the city, which was looted and torched.

Opposite and right: Wat Phra Ram and Wat Chai Wattanaram at Ayutthaya are both characterized by superb Khmer-style towers, known as *prang*.

CARVED IN STONE

King Ramkhamhaeng of Sukhothai is credited with the creation of the Thai alphabet, in which he recorded the history of his kingdom in a famous stone inscription of 1292. In what is assumed to be his own words, Ramkhamhaeng described most notably Sukhothai's prosperity and the paternal nature of his rule: 'There is fish in the water and rice in the fields … When commoners or men of rank differ and disagree, [the King] examines the case to get at the truth and then settles it justly for them.'

It is this, along with innovative art and architecture, which has given rise to a popular sentiment common among Thais that the Sukhothai kingdom represented a golden era.

Ayutthaya never recovered from this devastating blow and was abandoned. Nonetheless, within just seven months the Thais rallied under the leadership of General, later King, Taksin and succeeded in expelling the Burmese. Taksin then founded a new Thai capital at Thonburi, on the west bank of the Chao Phraya River some 80 km (50 miles) downstream from Ayutthaya.

A contemporary of both Sukhothai and Ayutthaya, the northern kingdom of Lanna was founded in 1296 by King Mengrai. Of Thai and Lawa descent, Mengrai was the chieftain of a petty northern principality who first conquered the Mon state of Haripunchai (present-day Lamphun) and then other small Thai principalities to create a united kingdom centred on the town of Chiang Mai, which he built as his new capital.

In spite of wars with Burma and Ayutthaya, and periods of subjugation by both, Lanna succeeded in pursuing a largely autonomous development for over 600 years, and its art, architecture and other cultural distinctions remain apparent today. Only in 1939 did Lanna come under the full control of the central Thai government.

That government was and is focused on Bangkok. After the fall of Ayutthaya, King Taksin (ruled 1768–1782) reigned for 14 years from his capital at Thonburi, but his rule was seen as increasingly despotic and in a popular revolt he was overthrown by military commander General Chakri, who was crowned King Rama I and so became the first monarch of the current Chakri dynasty.

On assuming the throne, King Rama I relocated the capital across the Chao Phraya to Bangkok, at that time a small trading port on the river's east bank, as a defence against any possible attack out of Burma. Concentric canals were dug to connect with the river as a further defensive measure, and these effectively created an island (today known at Rattanakosin Island) on which the core of the city was to be built. Interconnecting canals were also dug to facilitate transportation, giving rise Bangkok's familiar description as 'The Venice of the East'. (The proper name bestowed on the capital by King Rama I ranks as the world's longest with 165 letters of which the first two syllables are *Krung Thep*, 'City of Angels'.)

Enjoying peace and stability, the first three reigns of the Chakri dynasty were devoted primarily to developing Bangkok with Ayutthaya as its model so as to reflect past glory and restore national pride. This retrospective and introspective stance was reversed during the fourth reign, when King Mongkut (ruled 1851–1868), of *The King and I* fame, looked to the West as he sought to modernize the nation. He negotiated foreign trade agreements, the first such foreign treaties since the 17th-century reign of King Narai, and set in motion far-reaching reforms.

King Mongkut was succeeded by his son, King Chulalongkorn, Rama V (ruled 1868–1910), who is revered as one of Thailand's greatest monarchs. He consolidated and greatly expanded the policies initiated by his father and during a reign of 42 years his enlightened rule initiated reforms and modernization on an unprecedented scale. New administrative, economic, judicial, educational and military systems were established during the reign, while material improvements included the first railways, electricity in Bangkok, and telegraphic and postal services.

Much of the change was inspired by Western models. Moreover, an interest in the West was all part of an astute and farsighted policy by which King Chulalongkorn sought, as had his father, to avoid the colonial fate that befell all of Thailand's neighbours by forging good relations with the major European powers, as well as by adopting social and commercial systems that would preclude any excuse for foreign aggression. This resistance to imperialism and assurance of national independence remains a source of pride to all Thais.

THE BOWRING TREATY

Negotiated by Sir John Bowring, envoy of Britain's Queen Victoria, the Bowring Treaty of 1855 was the first of the historic agreements between Siam and the major Western powers that granted generous trade concessions, as well as extraterritorial rights.

The lifting of the tariff and monopoly restrictions that Bowring secured heralded a new age of commerce and international relations for Siam. Similar treaties with other European powers, as well as the USA, followed shortly afterwards.

An enlightened monarch in every respect, King Rama IV was a keen astronomer and correctly predicted a solar eclipse, as commemorated by this statue (above) in Prachuab Khiri Khan.

The pattern of modernization and Westernization was continued under King Vajiravudh, Rama VI (ruled 1910–1925), the first Thai monarch to be educated overseas, in England at Oxford and Sandhurst. However, by the seventh reign, that of King Prajadhipok (ruled 1925–1935), the Thai economy was in poor shape, a situation aggravated by the financial crisis of the American and European markets in the early 1930s. This stimulated growing political dissent among a small group of military officers and civil servants, who staged a bloodless coup d'état in 1932 and called for a constitutional monarchy. King Prajadhipok accepted the demand, but strained relations with the new government led to his abdication in 1935, when he was succeed by King Ananda, Rama VIII (ruled 1935–1946).

Thailand's involvement in the Second World War was an ambivalent and reluctant one. In December 1941, the government, seeing that resistance would be futile, acquiesced to Japan's demand to allow passage for its troops through Thai territory and their continued presence in the country. Although Thailand declared war on Britain in January 1942, it was not effected in the USA, where the Thai ambassador, M.R. Seni Pramoj, refused to submit his government's declaration and instead set about forming a Free Thai movement, which supported the Allies and ensured that Thailand ended the Second World War on the side of the victors.

Tragedy struck the nation in 1946 when King Ananda was found dead of a gunshot wound at the Grand Palace in unexplained circumstances. He was succeeded by his brother, King Bhumibol Adulyadej, Rama IX, whose reign continues today as the longest in Thai history. Deeply loved and revered by the entire nation, King Bhumibol has shown extraordinary dedication to his people, initiating countless royal projects aimed at raising living standards, especially those of the rural poor. His reign also representing

stability as the country struggled to consulate its fledgling democracy in the second half of the 20th century, when military coups were almost seasonal.

With local communist insurgency suppressed and better relations established with its neighbours in the post-Vietnam War era, Thailand made considerable progress during the 1980s and 1990s in political, social and, not least, economic terms, with the country's economy growing at an unprecedented rate.

Above: Portraits of Thailand's much-loved present monarch, HM King Bhumibol Adulyadej, are widely displayed on the occasion of his birthday.

Above left: King Chulalongkorn, pictured here in a portrait in the Maha Chakri Throne Hall, remains one of the nation's most revered monarchs.

New-found wealth transformed Bangkok and other urban areas, as well as beach resorts, from the mid 1980s to the mid 1990s. The changes were evident both in physical terms, as with the wholesale construction of high-rise office towers and condominiums, 5-star hotels and luxury spas, championship golf courses and more, and in the social sphere with the emergence of a nouveau riche urban middle class and a vibrant youth culture. There was also a renewed national pride and a heightened sense of cosmopolitanism.

Even when the bubble burst in 1997, the Thais showed characteristic resilience in speedily bouncing back from the crash, and the social, political and cultural effects of new wealth and globalization became irreversible.

It was, of course, the urban population that had reaped most benefits in the 1980s and '90s, while conditions of the rural poor changed little. A golden opportunity for substantive national development came in 2001 when telecoms billionaire Thaksin Shinawatra and his Thai Rak Thai (Thai Love Thai) party won a landslide victory in the national elections. For the first time in the country's constitutional history the government had an absolute majority in parliament. However, in spite of introducing a number of populist policies, such as farm debt moratoriums and cheap healthcare, Thaksin's self-styled CEO form of government proved largely self-serving.

Thaksin was ousted by a military coup in 2006, with corruption cited as the justification. A Democrat-led coalition government was later formed, while Thaksin, living in self-exile, continued to play politics, inciting his still strong and loyal powerbase of rural poor to oppose the government.

Currently, Thailand is in a state of transition as two colour-coded factions (not political parties), the yellow-shirted People's Alliance for Democracy (PAD) and the Thaksin-inspired red-shirted United Front for Democracy Against Dictatorship (UDD), field mass demonstrations in support of their different agendas. During March–May 2010, the 'Red Shirts' held a prolonged demonstration in Bangkok demanding that the government step down. After attempts at negotiations failed, the demonstration was broken up by a military crackdown, and the physical and psychological damage suffered by the country was considerable.

There is a genuine argument for political change and social reform, although with personalities playing a greater role than ideologies, the outlook is uncertain. However, historically the Thais have always managed to resolve their problems in their own unique and inimitable way.

BOOM AND BUST

Thailand's boom from the mid-1980s to 1997 saw foreign investment in Thailand increased tenfold; manufacturing came to account for four-fifths of exports, compared to three-fifths originating from agriculture in 1980; the urban population and the average per capita income doubled in a decade.

When the inevitable bust came in mid-1997, over two million people lost their jobs, the Baht currency fell some 40 per cent against the US dollar, and the economy shrunk by 11 per cent. The crash, as summed up by historians Pasuk Phongpaichit and Chris Baker, resulted from 'the explosive chemistry' of mixing careless lending by international finance and 'the pirate instincts of Thai businessmen and politicians'.

Opposite above: Thailand's luxury beach resorts remain top tourist attractions in spite of recent political turmoil in the capital, Bangkok.

MODERN GOVERNMENT

Thailand is a democratic constitutional monarchy whereby a hereditary monarch is the head of state and an elected prime minister is the head of government.

Government is centralized in Bangkok and the National Assembly of Thailand, or Parliament of Thailand, consists of two chambers: an upper house of 150 senators and a lower house of 480 representatives (MPs).

For administrative purposes, the country is divided into 76 provinces (*changwat*), which are further divided into districts (*amphoe*), sub-districts (*tambon*) and villages (*baan*).

Economy

Thailand is an export-oriented emerging economy, with exports accounting for more than two-thirds of GDP and the major export markets being the USA, Japan, China, Singapore, Hong Kong and Malaysia. In terms of GDP per capita, the country ranks as the fourth richest among the nations of Southeast Asia after Singapore, Brunei and Malaysia.

Traditionally an agrarian society, Thailand remains the world's leading exporter of rice and a major exporter of shrimp, while other crops include coconuts, maize, rubber, soybeans, sugar cane and tapioca. However, although slightly more than half of the country's total population is still engaged in agriculture or agro-industries, manufacturing has become increasingly important in recent decades, with the main industries being textiles, electronics, cement and automobiles and automotive parts. The other vital sector of the economy is tourism, which accounts for around 6 per cent of GDP.

Above: Despite the huge economic gains of recent decades, Thailand still finds a place for simple fresh produce markets.

Top: A city on the move, Bangkok is the hub of all major commercial, industrial and financial activity in the country.

Opposite: Thailand is the world's largest exporter of rice, though agriculture has now been overtaken in economic importance by manufacturing.

Buddhism

Thailand is a firmly Buddhist country, with more than 90 per cent of the population professing and practising Theravada Buddhism, the national religion supported by some 30,000 Buddhist monasteries throughout the country and a religious community of about 250,000 monks.

As one contemporary Thai commentator has remarked, 'Buddhism has become so integrated with Thai life that the two are hardly separable. Buddhist influences can be detected in Thai lifestyle, mannerisms, traditions, character, arts, architecture, language and all other aspects of the Thai culture.'

One of the world's great living religions, Buddhism is, strictly speaking, atheistic in that it implies no question of faith nor demands any belief in the existence of a god. Essentially Buddhism is a way of life, a rational philosophy based on seeing, knowing, understanding and accepting worldly reality. It derives from the teachings of The Buddha, the 'Enlightened One', the title of a historical person who lived more than 2500 years ago.

The Buddha was born Siddhartha Gautama near Lumbini, in present-day Nepal, in the 6th century BC. He was the son of a king and grew up in his father's palace amid ease and luxury, all the time shielded from contact with the harsh realities of the world at large. One day, curiosity led him outside the palace, where he was shocked to see evidence of disease, old age and death.

Siddhartha was then 29 years old. His unexpected exposure to human misery made him determined to find a way to relieve mankind from suffering. He accordingly left his wife and child, renounced the riches of his birth and became an ascetic. After six years' wandering, he abandoned the extreme form of asceticism he had been following, electing instead a 'Middle Way' of moderation and meditation. It was while meditating, reputedly seated beneath a bo tree in the vicinity of Bodhgaya, northern India, that he attained enlightenment, supreme understanding of man's predicament.

The Buddha's insight into ultimate reality was embodied in the 'Four Noble Truths' – *dukkha* (suffering and its inevitability), *samudaya* (the cause of suffering which is desire), *nirodha* (the cessation of suffering through the extinction of desire) and *magga* (the way to the cessation of suffering, which is encompassed by the Noble Eightfold Path, namely: right understanding, right intention, right speech, right action, right livelihood, right effort, right mindfulness and right concentration).

Implicit in this understanding is a belief in the earlier Indian concept of reincarnation. Thus the ultimate aim of Buddhism is the release from the endless cycle of rebirth and suffering by extinguishing desire, which is to achieve the state of *nirvana*.

Above: A Buddhist monk sounds the temple bell at Wat Suwanaram, one of the most venerable temples in Phetchaburi.

THE BUDDHA IMAGE

The most widely seen and arguably the finest form of classical Thai art is the Buddha image. They are not, however, primarily aesthetic creations, nor are they idols, rather they are reminders of the teachings of the Enlightened One and, in theory at least, are all modelled on his attributes.

Images were executed in one of four basic postures – standing, sitting, walking and reclining – and in addition individual images display different mudras, or hand gestures. For example, both hands placed in the lap of the sitting Buddha indicate the meditation pose, whereas if the fingers of the right hand are pointing to the ground the statue represents the Buddha's subduing of Mara (forces of evil). In the standing image, the right hand raised signifies the mudra of 'Dispelling Fear'.

THE SUPERNATURAL IN THAI LIFE

Although Thais genuinely adhere to Buddhism, the religion is concerned primarily with man's ultimate release from suffering and as such it does not address mundane problems. At the same time, it is a tolerant faith, not necessarily excluding additional beliefs which may be deemed relevant to daily well-being.

Accordingly, the Thais have retained from their animistic ancestors a host of beliefs in spirits and supernatural powers which interact with ordinary life. The most visible manifestation of this is the spirit house found in the compound of virtually every building – domestic, commercial and government. These small, highly ornate structures, typically crafted in the form of a temple or traditional house and raised on a pillar, are intended as homes for the spirits that originally occupied the land.

Belief in supernatural powers is also witnessed in the wearing of various kinds of charms, amulets and magical tattoos, all of which are designed to protect the wearer from harm. A high regard for the auspicious is also widely held and many Thais will consult a fortune-teller before any important undertaking.

Above right: Files of saffron-robed monks walking in procession on their early morning alms round are a quintessentially Thai sight.

Opposite: Monasticism is central to Theravada Buddhism and most young Thai men will enter the monkhood for at least a short period.

The early form of Buddhism, known as Theravada or the 'teaching of the elders', was later challenged by a new school which aimed to have a more popular appeal. It called itself Mahayana, or 'Great Vehicle', as it offered salvation to a greater number of people than Theravada Buddhism. Mahayana Buddhism eventually spread to China, central Asia, Japan and other parts of east Asia, as well as to Vietnam, whereas Theravada Buddhism found a stronghold in Sri Lanka and was later to become the dominant faith in Burma, Laos, Cambodia and Thailand.

Today, Buddhism remains one of the underpinning concepts from which Thai society draws its quintessential strength. The monastic system persists and young men still enter the monkhood for at least a brief period once in their lives to earn merit for their parents as well as for their own spiritual development.

In the practice of Theravada Buddhism there is a distinction between the observances of the monk and those of the layman. The former strives for the cessation of desire and ultimate release from the cycle of death and rebirth, with meditation being the principle means of cleansing the mind and aiding concentration on the central aim of achieving nirvana.

For the ordinary person, the attainment of nirvana is beyond contemplation, and its pursuit is postponed to a future existence. Instead, the aim is to avoid evil and lead a good life based on self-control, restraint and meditation. By trying to lead a good life the layman has the opportunity to accrue merit which will ensure rebirth under more favourable conditions in the next incarnation.

Ways in which merit may be earned are many and various. Most typical and most visible is by giving food and other offerings to monks who make early morning alms rounds in cities, towns and villages throughout the country. Most people will also pray at temples, especially on major Buddhist festival days.

THE THAI TEMPLE

'They are gorgeous; they glitter with gold and whitewash … against that vivid sky, in that dazzling sunlight, they hold their own, defying the brilliancy of nature and supplementing it with the ingenuity and playful boldness of man.' So wrote Somerset Maugham in 1930. Most visitors to Thailand share this delight in Thai temples, though there is much more to admire than just their visual impact.

Firstly, 'temple' is largely unsatisfactory as a translation of the Thai word *wat*. It implies a single structure, as is the case with a Christian church, but this is not the case with a Buddhist *wat*. Besides monks' residential quarters that are commonly, though not always, found at a *wat*, a Thai temple is a complex comprising several distinct religious buildings.

The principal structure is the *bot*, the most sacred part of the temple and the place where monks' ordination ceremonies are conducted. A temple will also probably have one or more *viharn*, a hall similar in appearance to a *bot* but used as a sermon hall for monks and lay worshippers. Both structures follow identical architectural styles, being rectangular buildings with sweeping multi-tiered roofs covered with glazed orange and green or blue tiles. Each end of a roof's peak terminates in a gilded finial known as a *cho fa*, or 'sky tassel'.

The other characteristic temple structure is the *chedi*. Dominating the compound of a *wat*, this is a tall decorative spire constructed over relics of the Buddha, sacred texts or an image. Essentially there are two basic forms: bell-shaped and raised on square or round terraces of diminishing size, and tapering to a thin spire, or a round, finger-like tower.

Other buildings in a temple compound can include a library for sacred texts, and a *mondop*. Traditionally the former was built on stilts over a pond to protect the fragile manuscripts from ants, while the *mondop* is a square building with a tapering roof enshrining some relic, often a Buddha footprint, a decorated stone impression far larger than life-size.

Above right: The lines of the steep roof of Viharn Phra Mongkol Bophit in Ayutthaya is dictated by the huge Buddha image enshrined within.

Right: Wat Phra That Phanom, in Nakhon Phanom province, is notable for its square-shaped Laotian-style *chedi*, known as a *that*.

Opposite: Most often seen are bell-shaped *chedis*, as pictured here at Wat Phra That Haripunchai in Lamphun, which are of Sri Lankan influence.

The Arts

Buddhism provides the single most important inspiration for the arts of Thailand, and Buddhist sculpture and temple mural painting are the two most accomplished classical art forms. By contrast, a third major art form, dance drama, along with its related art of puppet theatre, is secular in content.

Sculpture

Although sculptors adhered to the essential conventions of Buddhist iconography, stylistic differences did occur and various schools of sculpture flourished during different periods of Thailand's history, resulting in statues displaying distinct stylistic qualities. In the pre-Thai period, the three principal civilizations of Dvaravati, Khmer and Srivijaya all produced exquisite artworks, Hindu and Buddhist sculptures, each with its own characteristic style.

Typically produced in stone or terracotta, early Dvaravati Buddha sculptures are heavily influenced by Indian styles, while later images are less massive and have a more indigenous look as evidenced by a flatter face, broader nose and thicker lips. Srivijaya images differ from those of Dvaravati in that they reflect the Mahayana, rather than Theravada, tradition of Buddhism. Thus Bodhisattvas (Buddhas-to-be) were more widely portrayed, while notable among the later Srivijaya period are images of the Buddha seated beneath a *naga* (mythical snake).

Khmer art, also referred to as Lopburi art in Thailand, has Buddha images both carved in stone and cast in bronze, and typical characteristics are the cranial protuberance modified into three rows of lotus petals, and a lotus bud halo. As Mahayana Buddhism was dominant with the Khmer, statues of the Buddha in royal attire, which includes a diadem and jewellery such as earrings and necklaces, were common at this time.

The first of the Thai schools of sculpture, that of Sukhothai, produced images that were far more stylized than anything that had gone before, being marked by a greater fluidity in the line of the body and an uncanny degree of serenity and spirituality expressed in the facial features Principle characteristics are a tall flame halo, small hair curls, oval face, arched eyebrows, hooked nose and a smiling expression.

In the north, the art of the Lanna kingdom, generally referred to as Chiang Saen style, falls into two basic groups: early and late. The images of the former type exemplify Indian Pala styles which were probably inherited from Haripunchai (present-day Lamphun), which was conquered by Lanna. Distinctive characteristics are a halo in the form of a lotus bud, a round face, prominent chin and a stout body with a well developed chest.

The later period, at its height during the reign of the Lanna King Tilokaraja (ruled 1441–1487), coincided with the blossoming of Theravada Buddhism in the north and shows both Sukhothai and Sri Lankan influences in the flame halo, oval face and more slender body of the Buddha images.

In central Thailand and becoming gradually dominant throughout the Kingdom, the art of Ayutthaya again divides into two categories, that of U-Thong (12th–15th centuries) and Ayutthaya proper which lasted until the mid-18th century.

U-Thong images passed through stages when Dvaravati, Lopburi and Sukhothai styles in turn dominated, though they are essentially typified by a square face and a stern expression. In the Ayutthaya style proper, the heritage of Sukhothai came to outweigh that of the Khmer, but the U-Thong form never completely vanished and the Buddha images of this period are scarcely comparable to the achievements of Sukhothai's Golden Age. Some distinction was achieved, however, in the late Ayutthaya period when Buddhas

in royal attire were popular, although the decoration is more distinguished than the portrayal of features.

The current period of Thai sculpture, that of Bangkok which dates from 1782, displays little innovation, although one masterpiece from the reign of King Rama III (ruled 1824–1851) is the giant statue of the reclining Buddha enshrined at Wat Po. This is an extraordinarily serene image in spite of its massive size that tends to overpower normal aesthetic appreciation.

Above: An image in early Chiang Saen style at Wat Chama Thevi in Lamphun with characteristic round face and stout body.

Above left: The Buddha seated beneath a *naga*, as in this statue at Wat Chedi Chet Thaeo, Si Satchanalai, is typical of the Srivijaya period.

Opposite: Buddha images of the Sukhothai period display great fluidity of line and a superb sense of serenity.

Mural Painting

Buddhism also informs Thai classical painting, the art form that achieved its finest expression in temple murals. Typically these were painted on all four walls of *bots* and *viharns*, though due to the fragile nature of the medium and the ravages of the climate few examples survive from before the 18th century.

All murals were purely didactic in purpose and the classic formula was to decorate the side walls with episodes from the life of the Buddha or his previous incarnations, individual scenes being separated by registers of praying celestial beings. The back wall generally showed a graphic interpretation of the Buddhist cosmology, and the front wall was covered with the scene of Buddha's victory over Mara (the forces of evil).

Typically, murals lack any attempt at depicting perspective and figures tend to be small, while the entire picture area is 'busy' and

Puppet Theatre

Among the earliest of Thai performing arts was the *nang* shadow play. The name literally means 'hide' or 'skin', and the performance is created by the manipulation of cut-out buffalo-hide figures held aloft on two sticks and presented as transparencies against an illuminated screen. This type of theatre probably originated in India and eventually found its way to Thailand via Java sometime in the 15th century.

The *nang yai* (literally 'large hide') form of the play takes its story directly from Thailand's national epic the *Ramakien*, and several hundred cut-out figures depict single and paired characters against intricate backgrounds of palaces, landscapes and other scenes. A full performance would take some 720 hours to stage, and commonly a selection of episodes, or 'sets', of proven popularity constituted a single show.

Today, *nang yai* is a dying art and performances are rarely staged, although shadow puppetry, *nang talung*, which uses smaller silhouettes with movable parts, can still be seen at local festivals in southern Thailand.

An allied classical entertainment, also now sadly in decline, is that of *hun krabok* puppet theatre. Featuring minutely detailed marionettes representing characters from the *Ramakien*, *hun* puppets are operated by strings from below and skilfully manipulated to imitate with amazing faithfulness the actions of *khon* dancers.

filled with detail. Because of the latter convention, artists often completed backgrounds with scenes of Thai daily life that are fascinating for their content and as areas where the painters are able to display greater self-expression.

Above: Murals at Wat Phumin, Nan, depict episodes from the Buddha's lives, though settings are seen through the eyes of Lanna artists.

Opposite above: Late Ayutthaya-period murals often made used of graphic dividers to separate rows of celestial worshippers.

Opposite below: A charming detail from Wat Phumin shows young Lanna men and women in 19th-century dress.

Above: An acknowledged master of shadow puppetry, Suchart Subsin strives to keep the art alive at his workshop in Nakhon Si Thammarat.

Dance Drama

Leaving aside folk and regional dances, the two major forms of Thai classical dance drama are *khon* and *lakon nai*. In the beginning both were exclusively court entertainments, and it was not until much later that a popular style of dance theatre, *likay*, evolved as a diversion for the common folk who had no access to the exclusive world of royal performances.

Both *khon* and *lakon nai* are strictly classical and highly stylized in nature. Each is a distinct form of dance drama, although there are shared aspects that distinguish Thai theatre in general.

The more famous of the two is *khon* which is a masked dance dramatization of the *Ramakien*, the Thai version of the Indian *Ramayana* epic, a moral tale concerning the struggles of Prince Rama and Hanuman's monkey army against the forces of evil. Developing out of shadow-play in the 16th century, a full *khon* performance demands a vast cast of actors playing the roles of gods, giants, men, monkey warriors and assorted beasts. All the characters were at one time depicted by actors wearing elaborate masks, but in latter-day shows only the masks of giants and animals have been retained. Nevertheless, any narrative is still left to a chorus, and actors keep their faces expressionless, communicating solely through a complex vocabulary of hand gestures and body movements.

Whereas *khon* portrays exclusively the *Ramakien* story, *lakon nai* may take its narrative content from a variety of legends, the *Inaw*, another princely tale, being one of the most popular. A further difference is that masks are not worn by *lakon nai* dancers.

Traditionally *lakon nai* was danced exclusively by women and the *khon* only by men. Such a division between the sexes is no longer strictly adhered to, but it does point to a more vital distinction between the two dramatic styles. While both forms rely on gesture and posture as modes of expressing emotion as well as action, there is a fundamental difference in emphasis. Whereas the *khon* actor seeks virtuosity in strength and agility and muscular exertion, the *lakon nai* dancer is persuasive through grace and remarkably controlled movement. Each traces intricate patterns of motion through the use of hand, arm and the studied raising and lowering of the body, yet the male's movements are emphatic and staccato in execution while the female's are more fluid and subtly beguiling.

Music is integral to all forms of Thai dance drama and *khon* and *lakon nai* performances are accompanied by an orchestra comprising traditional instruments. Small bell-like cymbals are used to set the pace while the music of the rest of the orchestra lends mood. Like most other aspects of classical Thai theatre, the orchestra is bound by convention. Essentially the tunes are indicative of specific actions and emotions, so there are 'walking tunes', 'marching tunes', 'laughing tunes', 'weeping tunes', 'anger tunes' and so on.

If *khon* and *lakon nai* can be compared as art to Western ballet, *likay* is the equivalent of pantomime. In form, it basically parodies *lakon nai* (though its origins also owe something to Chinese opera), and the dramatic content is standard, full of the tried and tested stuff of melodrama, although improvisation plays an important part, and performances can differ markedly depending on the quickness of the actors' wit. Puns, verbal virtuosity and slapstick humour are *likay*'s stock-in-trade.

THE *RAMAKIEN*

It sounds a heady brew. 'A work combining the popularity of the Arthurian legends, the literary force of the works of Shakespeare and the authority of the Bible.'

Thus one art historian sums up the *Ramakien*, the epic tale that has shaped classical Thai arts more than any other secular influence. It provides story lines for dance drama, puppet plays and shadow theatre, as well as the pictorial world of murals, bas reliefs, sculpture and the decorative arts.

Derived from the Indian *Ramayana* epic, reputedly written some 2000 years ago and accredited to the Indian poet Valmiki, the *Ramakien* opens with the founding of the rival cities of Ayutthaya, capital of the gods, and Langka, city of the demons. The long and convoluted tale revolves around the struggle between these two opposed forces, the principal action focusing on the trials and tribulations of Ayutthaya's Prince Rama, the abduction of his wife, Sita, and the eventual defeat of Langka by Hanuman and his army of monkey warriors.

Like all the best stories, the *Ramakien* combines adventure and excitement – plus a touch of comic relief – with moral edification. At the same time, full play is given to strange occurrences in which magic, divination and other mysteries are important elements.

Above: The vocabulary of classical dance drama is one of graceful hand gestures and body posture while fabulous costumes create a spectacle.

Opposite above: Young performers enjoy time out for a meal between shows of national and regional folk dances.

Opposite below: A scene from a classical dramatic performance staged during a temple fair at Bangkok's Wat Arun, Temple of Dawn.

Food

Thais are great eaters. That's not to say that they overeat, but they do relish their food, appreciating individual tastes and the subtle combinations of dishes with a gourmet's delight.

Freshness of ingredients is fundamental to Thai cooking, and in this respect the country is fortunate in that the land, rivers and seas yield rich harvests. The staple food, rice, grows in abundance, as do the numerous varieties of green vegetables, tropical fruit, herbs and spices so beloved of the Thai palate. Pork and poultry are favoured meats, although many types of fish and shellfish, both freshwater and marine, are a traditional source of protein and are equally popular.

As with other cultural forms, Thai cooking has evolved over centuries and local ingredients and cooking styles have been augmented and developed though a mosaic of external influences. From China came noodles and stir-fries, curries were adopted from India and Myanmar, while that now characteristic ingredient, the chilli pepper, was most probably introduced by the Portuguese in the early 16th century.

As always, foreign influences were adapted with a distinct indigenous style so that the outcome was something fresh and different. Stir-fries, for example, are light and usually not thickened with cornflower as in China. Curries are based on a freshly pounded paste of herbs and spices rather than on dry flavourings as in India. Moreover, the blend of spices and herbs, along with the widespread use of coconut, are uniquely Thai.

Thais generally eat three meals a day (not counting those irresistible snacks from street vendors). Rice soup, *khao tom*, is traditional breakfast fare. Lunch, usually a hurried affair in these busy modern times, is generally one dish with rice or noodles. Dinner, on the other hand, is a substantial meal.

A typical Thai dinner consists of several dishes, which are served together and shared, with diners helping themselves to small servings from each plate as taste and appetite dictate, together with helpings from a communal bowl of plain boiled rice (sticky rice in the north and northeast).

Balance of the five fundamental tastes – spicy, sour, sweet, salty and bitter – are vital, as are textures, colours and visual presentation, and there are many ways to combine recipes in one meal. A traditional menu could, for example, consist of a steamed dish, a grilled or stir-fried dish, a soup (not a separate course as in the West), a curry or stew, a spicy salad and a vegetable dish. Dessert could be fresh fruit or a *kanom*, a sweet cake.

Fork and spoon are the preferred utensils, the fork being used to heap food onto the spoon (it is considered bad manners to eat from the fork, in the same way as people in the West frown upon putting a knife into one's mouth). As for drink, wine has become popular today among middle class Thais, although Thai beer or whisky (more like a sweet rum than Scotch) with water or soda goes well with the food.

Besides the rice and main dishes, absolutely essential to any Thai meal are the sauces to give additional spice and seasoning. For the novice there can be a bewildering number of these, but the most common are *nam pla*, a liquid fish sauce which is extremely salty, and *nam prik*, also a liquid but containing pieces of chillies, garlic, shrimp curd, sugar and lime.

Thais generally prefer hot, spicy food, but it is a misconception that all Thai dishes are equally fiery. Nonetheless, much of the appeal of Thai cuisine is derived from its seasoning which is integral to the culinary art. Red and green chillies of a dozen kinds are but one of many different ingredients that are combined to give a unique blend of flavours. Lemongrass, garlic, ginger, nutmeg, cloves, coriander, turmeric and other herbs and spices all have a role to play.

With regards to types of dishes, Thailand's greatest culinary contribution is undoubtedly *tom yam*. This is a sour soup, which can be made with various kinds of meat or fish, but its most famous version is with prawns, *tom yam goong*. The basic broth is flavoured with lemongrass, citrus leaves, lime juice, fish sauce and hot chillies.

Left: Freshly caught seafood, as displayed here at the Night Market in Hua Hin, features in some of the most appetizing Thai dishes.

Opposite: The Thai culinary art is all about harmony and the subtle blend of both main ingredients and a huge variety of seasonings. Pictured clockwise from top left are beef salad with chicken soup, *tom yam goong*, and food preparation at the Floating Market.

Chapter Two

Bangkok

City of Angels

A city of temples and palaces, of golden spires and orange tiered roofs, of saffron-robed monks and serene Buddha images. Equally a city of office towers and condominiums, of concrete and glass curtain walls, of business-suited executives and traffic-snarled streets. Bangkok can be all things to all people. Essentially a paradox, a seemingly impossible blend of old and new, of traditional Oriental splendour overlaid with a modern Western veneer, the Thai capital defies easy definition.

Opposite above left: Noisy and open to traffic fumes, the three-wheeled tuk tuk taxis are nonetheless popular and very much a part of the Bangkok cityscape.

Above left: With its distinctive spires, Wat Arun, Temple of Dawn, located on the west bank of the Chao Phraya River, symbolizes Bangkok's exoticism.

Opposite left: The statue of the Hindu god Brahma at Bangkok's Erawan Shrine is widely believed to bestow good fortune and attracts hundreds of devotees daily.

Left: Lumpini Park provides a welcome green oasis in the heart of Bangkok, a city increasingly dominated by the high-rise.

Bangkok

"…it's best to view Bangkok as a collection of separate districts, each with its own identity and ambience…"

The modern cityscape, reminiscent variously of Tokyo, Los Angeles or Chicago, bristles with luxury hotels, ritzy shopping plazas, Western fast-food outlets, cyber cafes and all the other trappings of a 21st-century city on the move.

Amazingly, in the wake of massive modern development, Bangkok retains its essence. It may in part echo other cities but an immutable Thainess nonetheless prevails so that Bangkok is Bangkok in the same way as Gertrude Stein's rose was a rose was a rose; it captivates by being simply itself.

The place is, as Pico Iyer has remarked, 'impossible to resist', although that doesn't necessarily make orientation any easier and Bangkok can baffle the first-time visitor.

Located on the east bank of the Chao Phraya some 20 km (12 miles) upstream from the river's outlet into the Gulf of Thailand, Bangkok is the nation's capital in every sense of the word. It is where the Royal Family resides, it is the seat of government and administration, and it is the focal point for virtually all major industrial, commercial and financial activity. It is also the country's main port, aviation gateway and home to in excess of one-tenth of the country's total population.

In spite of its paramount importance, the city's landscape is unprepossessing. It stretches out like an urban pancake laid out on a flat alluvial plain and lacks any obvious downtown area. Now that canals are no longer the main means of getting around, even the river is not a handy point of reference as, in the pattern of traditional riverine settlements, it is mostly fronted by buildings without public access.

To make sense of what can seem a tantalizing city, it's best to view Bangkok as a collection of separate districts, each with its own identity and ambience, which have merged to become a metropolis that is to a greater or lesser extent a definable entity. Since Bangkok evolved mostly by lateral expansion rather than by rebuilding on existing sites, these districts illustrate to a large extent the pattern of historical development.

Left: Khao San Road has been hugely successful in transforming itself into a haven for backpackers.

Opposite above left: Traversed by the Skytrain mass transit system, modern Bangkok continues to thrust ever upwards.

Opposite above right: A city of contrasts, Bangkok combines the classical, as with this statue of a mythical *kinnari,* figures that are half-bird, half-woman at Wat Phra Kaeo, with the contemporary.

Opposite below: Longtail boats are a fast way of navigating the Chao Phraya River, which remains an important transportation link.

Rattanakosin Island

When it was founded as the Thai capital in 1782, Bangkok could boast little more than a customs post and a fort that was the frontline defence against possible enemy shipping coming up the Chao Phraya River. When King Rama I mapped out plans for his new capital, it was his intention to build a city that would fully reflect the lost glory of the previous principal city, Ayutthaya. Bangkok, like its predecessor, was transformed into an island city, Rattanakosin, by the cutting of canals. Similarly, the focal point would be a royal palace complex, a city within a city that historically served as the symbolic – as well as the physical – heart of the nation.

Although simply known as the Grand Palace, this hub of old Bangkok is not a single structure but a collection of regal and administrative apartments, as well as site of the nation's most important temple, Wat Phra Kaeo (Temple of the Emerald Buddha), all encompassed in an area of nearly one square mile and surrounded by high crenellated walls.

The Grand Palace served as the official royal residence until the 20th century and during each of the first five reigns of the Chakri dynasty new buildings in varying styles were added to the complex. Hence one of the largest and most eye-catching of the royal apartments, the Chakri Maha Prasat Throne Hall, is a melding of Thai and European styles. Designed by English architect John

Clunish in what can be loosely described as Victorian Italianate style, it mixes arched windows and classical columns with traditional carved gables, gilded decorations and elongated roof spires.

However, it is the oldest structures that epitomise Thai classical architecture and make the Grand Palace everyone's dream of oriental splendour. Typical is the Dusit Maha Prasat Throne Hall, originally built in 1784 but later struck by lightning and reconstructed on a smaller scale. Modelled on one of Ayutthaya's finest royal halls, this building is exquisite in its multi-tiered tiled roof topped by an intricately decorated seven-tier gilded spire.

Above: In its architectural forms and stunning decorative detail the Temple of the Emerald Buddha inspires an inescapable sense of awe.

Opposite: The compound of the Temple of the Emerald Buddha is a veritable menagerie of mythical creatures, here a *kinnara* (half-man, half-bird).

Above: Wat Po offers a fine example of how intricate surface decoration is integral to classical Thai temple architecture.

Above right: Buddha statues line the cloisters of Wat Po, the individual images being a reminder of the Lord Buddha's teachings.

Opposite above: The 19th-century Chakri Maha Prasat Throne Hall at the Grand Palace is a glorious melding of Thai and European architectural styles.

Though the palace buildings are intriguing in their richness and variety they are completely outshone by Wat Phra Kaeo, which enshrines the Emerald Buddha. Set within its owned walled compound this, like the palace itself, is a complex of structures, of temple halls, pavilions, *chedis* and an array of statuary of weird and wonderful mythological creatures. From a distance the site is marked by the huge gilded Phra Si Rattana *chedi*, while within it is the *bot* that dominates.

This is Thailand's holiest temple and commands due respect as such, yet from a secular point of view it is the country's finest showcase of Rattanakosin-era art and architecture. From its marble base with a series of gilded bronze *garudas* (mythical half-bird, half-human creatures) to its walls covered in shimmering coloured glass and ceramic mosaic, doors and window shutters adorned in variously mother-of-pearl inlay and gilt-on-lacquer, and its tiered roof, here is a truly dazzling sight in which surface decoration is characteristically integral to the architectural design.

The interior is equally breathtaking, with mural paintings, Buddha statues and, high on its elaborate altar, the image of the Emerald Buddha, smaller than people expect, yet nonetheless imposing. What is perhaps most remarkable of all is that the mass of decorative detail does not overpower, and an almost palpable sense of religious awe and air of serenity prevails.

Many other classical monuments are to be seen in the area of Rattanakosin Island, not least Wat Pho (officially Wat Phra Chetuphon). Located next to the Grand Palace, this is Bangkok's oldest and largest temple complex, best known for its 46-m (150-ft) long statue of the Reclining Buddha, but also a wonderful example of a temple's historical role as a storehouse of knowledge (Wat Pho is still a centre for traditional medicine and massage).

THE EMERALD BUDDHA

Not made of emerald but carved from a single piece of green jasper, the 66-cm (26-in) tall statue of the Emerald Buddha, dressed in one of three costumes changed according to the three seasons in a solemn royal ceremony, is the nation's most sacred image and palladium.

According to legend, the statue was discovered in 1434 in the northern city of Chiang Rai when lightning split open an ancient *chedi*. Upon learning of this mysterious discovery, the King of Lanna ordered the statue to be brought to Chiang Mai, but the journey was unexpectedly protracted as the elephant bearing the image refused to travel the route. This was taken as an omen and instead the Emerald Buddha was taken to Lampang, where it resided for 32 years before finally being enshrined at Wat Chedi Luang in Chiang Mai.

Later, in 1552, a prince of Chiang Mai removed the statue and took it to Laos, and it was not until 1778 that General Chakri (later King Rama I) defeated the Lao and brought the Emerald Buddha back to Thailand.

A copy of the Emerald Buddha (right) is enshrined at Wat Phra Kaeo in Chiang Rai, the city where the image was first discovered.

Then across the Pramane Ground, the site of royal cremations and more commonly a public recreation area, the National Museum houses one of Southeast Asia's largest and most comprehensive collections of artefacts that offers an invaluable introduction to Thailand's history, as well as its arts and crafts.

On the far eastern edge of Rattanakosin Island rises the Golden Mount, a gilded *chedi* set upon a square sanctuary atop a massive concrete base. It may lack the architectural grace of other Rattanakosin-era monuments, but it is notable partly as a phenomenon – merely to have raised such an imposing structure on the soft alluvial soil of the Chao Phraya floodplain was an achievement – and partly for the panoramic views that vividly show how Rattanakosin Island has been preserved as a low-rise zone.

Thonburi

Stepping back further in time, across the Chao Phyra River from Rattanakosin Island is Thonburi, Bangkok's short-lived predecessor and now a part of the Greater Metropolitan area. Today the district is mostly suburban and its moment of glory was so brief as to leave little evidence. Thonburi does, however, boast a few interesting temples, the most famous being Wat Arun (Temple of the Dawn). Dating from the Bangkok period, this is virtually a city icon, and its unmistakable finger-like spire (*prang*), tiered terraces and coloured porcelain decoration present a classic image on the banks of the Chao Phraya.

But if Thonburi lacks monuments to its past, it has kept more of its old canals than Bangkok proper and touring these backwaters by longtail boat gives a glimpse of how the city must have looked when it was the 'Venice of the East'. It is not just the canals and the houses facing them that capture this atmosphere, but the lifestyles too – monks going on morning alms rounds, vegetable sellers, even a savings bank making collections, all by boat.

Above: The imposing *chedi*-topped Golden Mount on Rattanakosin Island was until the modern era Bangkok's tallest structure.

Opposite: An air of tranquillity and order pervades the well-tended compound of Wat Arun, Temple of the Dawn.

Above: Wat Suthat is one of Bangkok's most notable temples, not least because of its superb mural paintings.

Right: Thai temples are such wondrous sights that it is easy to forget the important role they play in the spiritual lives of the people.

Opposite: Carved foreign soldiers on the gates of Wat Ratchabophit hint at the temple's extraordinary mix of architectural and decorative styles.

Dusit

Northeast of Rattanakosin Island is Dusit, the location of Chitrlada Palace, the present official residence of the Royal Family, and of Ban Phitsanulok, the official residence of the Prime Minister. This modern-day royal and political heart of the nation is different in look and tone from the old city and clearly the product of a shift in Bangkok's development.

Broad avenues, tree-shaded *khlongs* (canals), buildings of Edwardian elegance and grand vistas unobstructed by even a shadow of a high-rise, all enhanced by a prevailing air of calm; it's not a picture of Bangkok that immediately springs to mind, and yet it is surprisingly characteristic of Dusit, created by King Chulalongkorn (Rama V) in the late 19th and early 20th centuries.

Remarkably, given Bangkok's rapid development in recent decades, much of Dusit today appears as its creator intended, preserving the grace and charm of an era marked by as radical a period of change as ours, but informed by an aesthetic sensibility as pronounced then as it is mostly lacking today.

Inspired by Western models not only in political and administrative reform but also in aesthetics, King Chulalongkorn sought both to modernize his capital and glorify it through monumental building that incorporated Western designs and technology. Various European architects were invited to Bangkok, many of them Italians, including Carlo Allegri, Annibale Rigotti and J. Grassi, but also English designers, such as John Clunish. They designed new buildings or offered advice on their construction. As a result, Bangkok's physical appearance was greatly altered.

Dusit was planned as a green city, spacious and majestic with residences for the King and his family laid out in landscaped grounds. To connect this new royal city to the Grand Palace, King Chulalongkorn commissioned the construction of Ratchadamnoen Avenue, based partly on the Champs Elysées in Paris and partly on London's The Mall. From the end of this grand boulevard another superb avenue, Ratchadamnoen Nok, swept straight as an arrow down to the Ananta Samakhom Throne Hall.

Today, Ratchadamnoen Avenue retains its grand proportions though its look has been spoilt by the rather severe architectural style of buildings put up in the 1930s and 1940s, along with the emotive but inelegant Democracy Monument slap in the middle. Ratchadamnoen Nok, on the other hand, is still a lovely tree-lined avenue, its air of genteel order and calm standing in marked contrast to most of Bangkok's other main thoroughfares.

Of the buildings to be seen today in Dusit, three in particular remain major landmarks. Firstly, Wat Benchamabophit stands as one of Bangkok's best known and most beautiful temples, the most outstanding of King Chulalongkorn's architectural contributions to the city. Commissioned in 1901, it is the last major temple to have

been built in the capital and, in keeping with the times, it filters traditional Thai design through 19th-century European styles.

Western borrowings are, however, restrained and the familiar form of traditional Thai religious architecture is retained to give an overall impression of classical elegance freshly interpreted. What is alien, however, is the principal construction material, white Carrara marble, which gives the temple its popular name, the Marble Temple. Enhanced by Wat Benchamabophit's isolated position in an unusually open site, it is this marble that gives a sense of solidity and permanence, and a formalism quite unlike that found at any other Thai temple.

The impact of Western influence is reflected inside the temple, where the murals differ from those of the past in both painting style and subject matter, the latter extraordinary for lively depictions of activities and achievements of the Fourth and Fifth reigns.

Above: Dating from the turn of last century, Wat Benchamabophit, the Marble Temple, possesses a beauty uniquely its own.

Right: Monks gather outside Wat Benchamabophit in the early morning to receive alms from the public.

Opposite: Ratchadamnoen Nok Avenue runs in a perfect straight line down to Italianate-style Ananta Samakhom Throne Hall, which once served as the National Parliament.

Of secular buildings in the Dusit area, quite the loveliest is Vimanmek Palace, a three-storey mansion made entirely of gold teakwood, the largest construction of its kind in the world. Although part of King Chulalongkorn's new palace complex, Vimanmek was originally built as a royal vacation residence on the island of Si Chang, located off the eastern seaboard, and then, in 1901, dismantled and reassembled in Bangkok, where it became the favourite retreat of King Rama V and his family. Aside from its architecture, the building is distinguished as the first in Bangkok to have electricity and an indoor bathroom.

The third of Dusit's major monuments, the Ananta Samakhom Throne Hall, is the most extravagant of all the Fifth Reign's European-inspired buildings. The domed structure loosely follows the classic Italian Renaissance style of St. Peter's in Rome, while the basic form is adorned with a wealth of friezes, Corinthian capitals, statuary and other ornamental detail. The interior matches the exterior in splendour, richly decorated in the grandest European fashion with works overseen by Italian painters such as Galileo Chini, Cesare Ferro and Carlo Rigoli.

Top: With 81 rooms spread over three storeys, Vimanmek Palace is the world's largest building made entirely out of golden teakwood.

Above: Beautifully restored as part of the 1982 Bangkok bicentennial celebrations, Vimanmek Palace is today one of the city's top sights.

Chinatown

It is not, of course, only the regal and the religious that define Bangkok; it was, and still is, a city of commerce and the needs of trade played their part in the city's growth, early on prompting another historical shift southeast from Rattanakosin Island running parallel to the Chao Phraya River. Until well into the 20th century, the river remained Bangkok's focal point and early expansion outside the royal city followed its banks, firstly with the development of what is still Chinatown, created when the traders and other original inhabitants of Bangkok were relocated downriver in order to make way for the construction of the Grand Palace.

Focused on Yaowarat Road and Sampeng Lane, Chinatown is set back from the river and forms a typically crowded district of narrow streets packed cheek by jowl with shophouses, workshops and market stalls. A large proportion of the commercial activity is ethnic in character – Chinese medicines, gold shops and such like – and apart from motorized traffic clogging the streets, Chinatown manages to preserve much of its original ambience.

Bounding one side of Chinatown is Charoen Krung (New Road) and although looking today like a typical Bangkok thoroughfare, it marks a fundamental turning point in the city's development. As

the name suggests, this was the capital's first paved road suitable for wheeled traffic and heralded the slow but inevitable demise of the river and its canals as the main communication and transportation arteries in and around the city.

Constructed in 1864, New Road follows a former elephant path and runs from the old royal city past Chinatown and on to what became Bangkok's foreign quarter and commercial hub for the big European trading houses, such as the East Asiatic Company, that were established in the latter half of the 19th century. Echoes of the heyday of this European quarter resound today in the riverside embassies of France and Portugal, Assumption Cathedral, Bangkok's principal Catholic church built in 1910, and, most famously, in the Mandarin Oriental Hotel, which is seen even now, with modern additions, as the city's finest hostelry and widely ranked among the best hotels in the world.

Above: Chinatown is almost as old as the city itself and, apart from motorized traffic and modern signage, it retains its typically ethnic character as a place of bustling trade and commerce.

Modern Bangkok

Road construction would eventually make Bangkok seem less like a Venice and more like a Los Angeles of the East as the motor car came to dominate. Even so the foreign quarter centred on New Road continued to boom until the Second World War. The Chao Phraya River also remained a focal point, but as the 20th century unfolded Bangkok increasingly turned its back on its traditional waterway as expansion headed eastward.

Not until the 1980s, when the growth of the tourism industry prompted a flurry of hotel construction and several of the new deluxe property developers realized that a river frontage offered a unique selling point, did some attention revert to the Chao Phraya. The move proved a success and today high-rise hotels and condominiums give a thrusting modern appearance to the river banks and the old foreign quarter.

There was, nonetheless, no halt to what was a rapidly increasing pace of expansion. In 1900 Bangkok's built-up area extended over 13.2 km² (5 sq miles); by 1936 this had more than tripled to 43.1 km² (16.6 sq miles). In 1960, the figure stood at 120 km² (46 sq miles), while today the greater metropolitan area measures more than 330 km² (127 sq miles). Paralleling the physical growth was a steady rise in Bangkok's population, from around 300,000 in 1900 to an unofficial figure today of more than 10 million.

Economic growth during the latter half of the 20th century led to an expansion of the business centre away from the banks of the river and into the Silom area, following communication lines which were originally canals. One example of this is Sathorn Road, a once gracious street divided by a tree-lined canal that today is an eight-lane thoroughfare running between a walled ribbon of murky water.

Silom Road itself, stretching from New Road to Rama IV Road and flanked by the roughly parallel roads of Sathorn and Suriwongse,

THAI BOXING

Thai boxing, Muay Thai, in which the feet, knees and elbows are used in addition to gloved fists, is Thailand's unique national sport, developed from an ancient style of martial art dating back to at least the early 15th century.

At its best it is a fast and furious contest between two superbly fit athletes, and it remains a hugely popular spectator sport. Bouts are staged most nights of the week in Bangkok at two stadiums, Lumpini on Rama IV Road, and Ratchadamnoen on Ratchadamnoen Nok Avenue in the Dusit area.

LUMPINI PARK

Bounded by Rama IV, Wireless, Rajdamri and Sarasin roads, Lumpini Park is Bangkok's 'lung', its green escape. Covering 57 ha (140 acres), the land was presented to the people in 1925 by King Vajiravudh (Rama VI), whose statue today stands opposite the park's main gates. After landscaping as a public recreation area, it was named Lumpini, in remembrance of the Lord Buddha's birthplace in Nepal, which was reputedly an enchanting garden.

With grassy expanses, trees, shrubs, two boating lakes and, most blissful of all, no traffic, this green oasis is popular with Bangkokians as an outdoor gym, and during the early morning it attracts large numbers of joggers and others performing their favourite forms of exercise from tai chi to ballroom dancing.

now has the city's single greatest concentration of offices, supported by department stores, hotels and other commercial, shopping and entertainment establishments, not least the notorious go-go bars of Patpong, to make it the closest to being downtown.

Leading east from Rama VI Road, opposite the Silom/Sathorn area, the major cross roads are Wireless, Rajdamri and New Rachadapisek. The area traversed by these is the greenest and least built-up sector of the modern city, encompassing Lumpini Park, the Royal Bangkok Sports Club and the artificial lake belonging to the Tobacco Monopoly of Thailand. Wireless Road itself, densely lined with old trees, stands in marked contrast to the city's more typical concrete canyons and preserves a sedate air.

Beyond is Sukhumvit Road, the main artery of Bangkok's eastern sector, the direction in which the city has expanded most since the mid-20th century. The area includes Ploenchit and Rama I roads, which are essentially continuations of Sukhumvit, and Phetchaburi Road to the northeast.

The first wave of sustained development was during the Vietnam War, when Phetchaburi in particular was a centre for US troops on R&R visits to Bangkok. Hotels, nightclubs and other entertainment spots mushroomed at that time, hastily constructed and without architectural distinction. From the mid 1970s onwards, however, the area has moved upmarket, primarily as a residential area but

Above left: Jim Thompson's House – the home of a legendary American adventurer and entrepreneur – is a fine example of traditional Thai domestic architecture wonderfully preserved in the heart of modern Bangkok.

Opposite: In little more than three decades Bangkok has transformed itself into a modern metropolis dominated by thrusting high-rises.

CHATUCHAK MARKET

Shopping is a big attraction for Thais and visitors alike, the latter drawn especially to Thai silk, gems and jewellery, tailor-made clothing, handicrafts, antiques and contemporary home décor items.

But main-street malls and smart shops don't have it all to themselves; Chatuchak Market, on the northern side of town, is famed for its thousands of stalls selling just about everything from antiques and clothing to porcelain, pets and plants. Open on Saturdays and Sundays, Chatuchak is a labyrinthine Aladdin's cave, a wonder in itself as much as for the wares it offers.

latterly also as a business, commercial and service centre. In the process a new vogue was created and the area now boasts some of the city's most upscale shopping malls, like the Emporium on Sukhumvit Road and Siam Paragon on Rama I Road.

Shopping, entertainment, and eating out are indeed the highlights of the Sukhumvit /Rama I area, and tourist sights are few, though not totally absent. Most striking is the Erawan Shrine on the corner of Rajdamri and Ploenchit roads. Here, amid the hubbub of one of the city's busiest traffic intersections, is a small but typically ornate shrine to the Hindu god Brahma, erected in the 1950s in the belief that it would ward off mishaps that were plaguing the construction of the adjoining Erawan Hotel (since redeveloped as the Grand Hyatt Erawan). Subsequently, the shrine earned a reputation as a source of good fortune, daily attracting hundreds of supplicants who make offerings and pray for all manner of blessings. If a blessing is granted, devotees may hire one of the resident classically attired dancers to perform as an expression of their gratitude. It is an arresting scene, visually dazzling and redolent with the scent of incense and floral garlands.

Equally unexpected on this modern side of town is Jim Thompson's House, located beside a canal at the end of a lane leading off Rama I Road. This is the former home of Jim Thompson, the American who revitalized the Thai silk industry in the 1950s and 1960s, now turned into a museum. The teakwood house, a superb example of traditional Thai domestic architecture, is an exhibit in itself, while displayed within is Thompson's fine collection of Asian antiques.

Aside from show pieces, such as Jim Thompson's House, traditional domestic architecture is a rarity today in Bangkok. In the last three decades, concrete and glass high-rises have reshaped the cityscape, along with flyovers and multi-lane expressways, while an elevated mass transit rail system and a subway have redefined how the city is experienced.

With few exceptions, Bangkok's modern architecture is uninspiring, tending towards what has been described as 'the fruit-salad school', whereby disparate forms, plucked from a spectrum ranging from Greek columns to glass curtain walls, can be found in a single structure.

Yet like all truly great cities, Bangkok is much more than the sum of its parts. Its changing face, its famous sights, its blend of old and new, all of its physical attributes are ultimately defined and coloured by the people. It is the quintessential Thai trait of *sanuk*, a sense of fun, of having a good time, that gives the city its unique flavour and irresistible charm. As Carol Hollinger wrote in her 1965 book *Mai Pen Rai Means Never Mind*, Bangkok 'would have seduced Calvin himself to gaiety'.

TRADITIONAL THAI HOUSES

Intended as a portable object, capable of being dismantled and reassembled at a new site, the traditional Thai house is a prefabricated structure, typically raised a couple of metres off the ground on sturdy pillars as protection against flooding. Walls comprise movable wooden panels attached to a superstructure of sturdy columns and beams.

Everything is held together with wooden pegs and rarely are nails used, making it easier to move house, literally. Wood-tiled roofs are steeply curved and given a broad overhang to provide protection from the bright sunlight and the monsoon rains. Outside and inside are linked by a verandah, an integral element in a dwelling where up to 60 per cent of the space is intentionally set aside for outdoor living.

Chapter Three

Beaches and Islands

Coastal and Southern Thailand

After Bangkok, Thailand is best know for its beaches and islands. It is these sun-drenched strands of white sand and idyllic isles that attract millions of visitors annually. Bangkok is a must-see, and while historical and cultural attractions elsewhere in the country do figure on the sightseeing list, no stay in the Kingdom is complete without at least a few lazy days by the sea.

Opposite above left: Calm, clear waters and dramatic scenery make the twin Phi Phi islands among the most popular of southern resorts.

Above left: Less well known than other beach destinations, the islands in Trang province provide an idyllic escape.

Opposite left: Krabi has it all, picture perfect with its combination of white sandy beaches, lush palm groves and soaring cliffs.

Left: With safe waters and always something to attract the attention, Thailand's beach resorts are perfect playgrounds for children.

Beaches and Islands

"… where Buddhist shrines cling to the cliffs … contrasted with the seaside vista … backed by rolling forested hills."

Like everything else in this land of contrasts, Thailand's beach resorts are not all of a type and you'll find they differ as much in character as in setting. Geographically, locations vary from the upper south and the east coast, both facing the Gulf of Thailand and readily accessible from Bangkok, and the more distant west and east coasts of the southern peninsula.

Upper South

Oldest of all Thailand's beach resorts and still a favourite as much among Bangkok residents as with foreign visitors is Hua Hin, situated, along with its seaside neighbour, Cha-am, on the upper west coast of the Gulf of Thailand, an easy drive less than 200 km (125 miles) south of Bangkok.

Both capitalize on the area's classic sweep of coastline, with Cha-am spread out along a casuarina-fringed shore that is virtually all beach, while Hua Hin boasts a majestic stretch of sand, separated at one end from a still active fishing village by a rocky headland and curving gently for some 5 km (3 miles) to its southern point where Buddhist shrines cling to the cliffs. Contrasted with the seaside vista is a green hinterland of mostly pineapple plantations backed by rolling forested hills that form the border with Myanmar.

Initially visitors to the western seaboard were few and regally distinguished. In August of 1868, King Mongkut first brought the region into focus when he journeyed a little way south of Hua Hin to observe a solar eclipse that he had predicted. Several European guests accompanied the royal party and were by all accounts duly impressed with both the scenery and the hospitality.

Later, American missionaries based at Phetchaburi, an important provincial centre north of Cha-am, were similarly impressed with the coast and made it a hot-season retreat, building the first bungalows on the beach. However, getting there was a tedious haul by canal boat and bullock cart, and it was not until the southern railway line was constructed in the early years of the 20th century that travel to the Western Gulf coast became not only easy but also fashionable.

Above: A pavilion at the summer palace of Phra Ratchaniwet Marukhathaiyawan, Hua Hin, leads directly to the water's edge.

Opposite above left: Boat trips around the uninhabited islands off the coast of Krabi afford the thrill of discovery.

Opposite above right: Hundreds of weird and wonderfully shaped limestone outcrops create a haunting seascape in Phang Nga Bay.

Opposite below: A standing Buddha image dominates the rocky headland of Khao Takieb at the southern end of Hua Hin.

It is said that when the route of the track was being planned, the railway surveyors were amazed by the sight of the magnificent beach at what was then known variously as Baan Samaw Riang or Baan Laen Him (Stony Point Village). The place was nothing more than a remote fishing village, but a station was constructed and opened on 25th November 1911. Shortly afterwards Prince Nares, a son of King Chulalongkorn, built a holiday palace at the beach and introduced the name Hua Hin, meaning 'Stone Head'.

With the development of the railway, the area became readily accessible, and other members of the Thai royal family and aristocracy joined Prince Nares in favouring Hua Hin as a retreat to escape from the stifling summers of Bangkok. In 1921, King Vajiravudh built a beachfront mansion and, five years later, his example was followed by his successor, King Prajadhipok, who built the palace he named Klai Kangwon, 'Far From Worries'.

Royal patronage of Hua Hin undoubtedly created a vogue, but it was the State Railways that assured the resort's wider popularity when it decided to build a hotel. As an indication of the esteem in which Hua Hin was held, this was planned as something vastly more luxurious than the simple rest houses then commonly found at halts along the railways of Thailand.

Opened in 1923, the Railway Hotel was a grand affair designed in Edwardian colonial style with huge rooms, airy verandahs and lavish use of teakwood. High standards were maintained from the start. The hotel's first housekeeper was no less a personage than the German-born wife of a Thai prince, and an English landscape gardener was commissioned to clip hedges into a fanciful topiary menagerie, a larger-than-life elephant being the pièce de résistance that is still maintained today.

Frequented by Bangkok's social elite, the Railway Hotel, together with the nearby 18-hole Royal Hua Hin Golf Course, opened in 1924, set the style that was to characterize Hua Hin for the next few decades. A guidebook published by the State Railways of Thailand in 1928 could proudly, and with justification, claim, 'Hua Hin-on-Sea, the famous seaside resort of Siam, with its excellent golf course, is most popular with travellers'.

Above: Hua Hin's regal tradition is most charmingly evoked by the railway station's elaborate royal waiting room.

Opposite: Complete with ponies for rides along the sands, Cha-am is very much oriented towards family seaside vacations.

ROYAL PALACES

The royal heritage of Hua Hin is brought vividly into focus at the magnificent summer palace of Phra Ratchaniwet Marukhathaiyawan, built in 1923 for King Vajiravudh. Designed by an Italian architect and constructed out of golden teakwood, the building is a dazzling composition of verandahs and latticework all styled in regal proportions. Now restored to its former glory, the palace captures the mood and style of a bygone era.

Continuing the royal association is Klai Kangwon (left), the palace built by King Prajadhipok (Rama VII), which is still used as a summer retreat by the present Royal Family. The public may visit the palace when the King is not in residence and the European-style buildings, as well as the glorious gardens, present a different, but equally fascinating, glimpse of Thai regal tradition.

GOLF

When the Royal Hua Hin Golf Course opened in the 1920s, a contemporary guidebook described it as 'second to none East of Suez'.

It may no longer merit that claim, though it remains as popular as ever, set as it is amid the rolling coastal hills where scenic vistas, most famously of a Buddhist temple halfway up a densely wooded slope near the 14th hole, match the sporting challenges of the 6654-yard, par-72 course.

Maintaining Hua Hin's golfing reputation are now half a dozen other championship-standard courses in the area, all of which boost Thailand's overall standing as a golfer's paradise.

After its heyday in the first half of the 20th century, Hua Hin languished until the 1980s, when it was discovered by a new generation. Modern holiday homes were built alongside the old sedate beachside bungalows and, most tellingly, a leading Bangkok architect designed Hua Hin's first condominium, introducing a style of accommodation that was rapidly gaining popularity in the capital. At the same time, the Railway Hotel was given a new lease of life when it was chosen as a set for the film *The Killing Fields* and given a facelift for a supporting role portraying Phnom Penh's leading hotel at the end of Cambodia's civil war.

Now the potential was there for all to see again. After its film debut, the Railway Hotel was taken over by a professional hotel chain (Sofitel Centara), greatly expanded and modernized but in such a way that its original ambience and gracious style were faithfully preserved.

Other developers also believed in Hua Hin's revival and new hotels offering excellent accommodation in many different styles have been built over the past couple of decades, spaced out along the coast from Cha-am all the way down to the rocky headland at Hua Hin's southernmost point. A good deal, but not all, of the new building is high-rise and has hence altered the profile of the shoreline, and yet a sense of nostalgia persists, as does a more typically Thai ambience than is found at some other resorts.

Long before the lure of the seaside focused attention on the shores of the Western Gulf, the region had achieved marked historical importance at Phetchaburi, 65 km (40 miles) north of Cha-am. Today the highway sweeps past the town and its treasures are ignored by most travellers who hurry by not wishing to be sidetracked on the way to the beach. And so Phetchaburi languishes as one of the most neglected destinations in the country.

Here history unfolds like the pages of a book, with major sights including the ruins of Wat Kamphaeng Laeng, a 13th-century Khmer temple, the superb late-Ayutthaya period temples of Wat Yai Suwannaram and Wat Ko Keo, both with fine, though sadly weathered, murals, and the 19th-century hilltop palace of Phra Nakhon Khiri, built by King Mongkut.

Opposite above: The hilltop palace of Phra Nakhon Khiri, in Phetchaburi, presents an intriguing collection of religious and secular buildings.

Opposite below: A quiet air envelops Phra Nakhon Khiri and its architectural interest is complemented by fine views.

South of Hua Hin and Cha-am, the attention shifts from history to the natural scenery of Khao Sam Roi Yot, ('Mountain of 300 Peaks') National Park. Covering some 100 km² (39 sq miles), the park encompasses a series of picturesque limestone outcrops rising above marshes, mangroves, untouched beaches and coves. It's a hauntingly beautiful spot and the 30-minute climb to the top of a signposted vantage point is worth it for the magnificent coastal panorama it affords.

Equally breathtaking are Sai, Kaeo and Phraya Nakhon caves. All three are fascinating caverns, weird and fabulous in their underground formations, while Phraya Nakhon has the additional charm of a Thai-style pavilion built in honour of King Rama V who visited the area in 1896.

Above: Dominated by the spires of Wat Mahathat, Phetchaburi is a small provincial capital packed with historical interest.

Opposite: Like a scene from an Oriental fairytale, a Thai pavilion stands in Phraya Nakhon cave in Khao Sam Roi Yot National Park.

East Coast

Across the Gulf of Thailand on Thailand's east coast, Pattaya is Hua Hin's opposite as much in character as in geography. Whereas Hua Hin is a triumph of provincialism, Pattaya, 145 km (90 miles) southeast of Bangkok, is an international playground, bold, brash and bawdy. As one guidebook puts it, 'You won't learn much about Thailand in Pattaya, but you could have quite a good time here.'

Unique in being a beach resort with city status, it bristles with hotels and is brimming with all manner of entertainment and sports packed into a couple of city blocks stretching inland from where jet skis buzz between tour boats riding at anchor and the rainbow canopies of parasails sweep across the sky.

Back in the 1960s, Pattaya was a quiet fishing village blessed with a majestic 4-km (2.5-mile) long sweep of beach fringing a perfect horseshoe bay. Vacationers from Bangkok found it an attractive weekend escape, prompting the beginnings of infrastructure development. Then, in the late 1960s and early 1970s, Pattaya was transformed as an R&R destination for American servicemen stationed in Thailand during the Vietnam War.

After the American involvement in Indochina ended, Pattaya was determined not to fall back into obscurity and it made an all-out attempt to attract another type of fun-and-sun-seeker – the international traveller. And it's never looked back. Colourful and buzzing with activity, it has evolved into a resort in a class of its own, offering more attractions in greater profusion than any other single destination in Southeast Asia.

Perhaps inevitably, by the late 1980s Pattaya had become a victim of its own success, suffering from over-building and a hopelessly strained infrastructure, while the less savoury nightlife attractions proliferated to give it an unfortunate, if not undeserved, reputation. But such is the irrepressible character of the place that the resort defied the pundits who wrote it off, and began revamping itself in the late 1990s.

Still if Pattaya is not to everyone's taste, travelling around the headland southeast of Pattaya into Rayong province brings you increasingly in touch with both a more traditional Thailand and more typical beach destinations.

Above: Parasailing in Pattaya Bay is just one of the resort's kaleidoscopic choice of activities to pursue on land, on the water and in the air.

Opposite: A resort with city status, Pattaya has a vibrant nightlife scene that more than rivals that of the capital itself, Bangkok.

ANCIENT CITY

Located just outside Bangkok in the direction of Pattaya, the Ancient City is a historical park with a fine collection of one-third-scale reconstructions of historical buildings from around Thailand.

It might sound like a typical tourist trap, but it is, in fact, extremely well done and presents an insightful picture of the Kingdom's architectural and cultural heritage relating to all parts of the country, with the layout of the 81-ha (200-acre) site roughly corresponding to the shape of Thailand itself.

The provincial capital is unexceptional, and the vacationer should head for the coast running between the fishing village of Ban Phe and the Laem Mae Pim headland near the town of Klaeng, a distance of about 20-25 km (12-15.5 miles) and virtually all of it beach.

The mainland beaches are complemented by offshore islands, the largest being Ko Samet, a thin sliver of land shaped roughly like a nail with a sloping flat head. Boasting some excellent beaches, today it is hugely popular with budget travellers and weekend excursionists from Bangkok. Ko Samet was immortalized by the classical Thai poet Sunthorn Phu, who set part of his epic *Phra Aphaimani* on the island, where the hero of the tale defeats a giant by playing a magic flute.

Southeast of Rayong lie Chanthaburi and Trat, the region's last two provinces before the border with Cambodia. Until recently both were famous sources of rubies and sapphires and while the local mines have now been largely worked out, Chanthaburi's provincial capital remains a renowned market for gems from all over Southeast Asia, which lends a buzz of excitement and colours the character of what is a fascinating town.

Adding further interest to Chanthaburi is its sizeable population of Vietnamese Christians who fled to the area in the 19th and first half of the 20th centuries to escape religious and political persecution. The influence of colonial Vietnam is readily seen in the town's French-style cathedral, the largest of its kind in Thailand, which was built in 1906 on the site of an 18th-century chapel.

Away from the town and the scarred earth of the open cast gem mines, Chanthaburi presents a lush landscape of low green hills, and much of the fertile land is given over to agriculture in the form of vegetable and fruit cultivation.

The major draw in Trat province is the island of Ko Chang, Thailand's second largest island after Phuket. Lying 8 km (5 miles) off the coast and measuring 30 km long by 8 km broad (19 by 5 miles) at its widest point, this is the main isle in a 52-island archipelago that forms Mu Ko Chang Marine National Park, established as a nature preserve in 1982.

The archipelago has a promising future as a tourist destination, and at the moment there is a precarious balance between the works of man and the natural environment. Ko Chang itself has a forested mountainous interior, while the coastline is fringed by small bays and excellent beaches.

Above left: Chanthaburi's French-style cathedral is the largest in Thailand.

Opposite above and below: The day's catch from fishing boats is brought to the fish market in Rayong.

THAI FRUITS

Exotic fruits are integral to everyone's idea of a tropical land, and Thailand more than fulfils expectation with an extraordinary variety of the juicy and succulent. A by-no-means exhaustive list includes:

Rambutan – distinguished by a hairy skin that when spilt reveals a crunchy sweet flesh around a woody seed.

Pomelo – belonging to the citrus family, this large yellowish-green globular fruit looks similar to a grapefruit and its tart, sweet flesh is segmented.

Mangosteen – this globular-shaped, thick-skinned fruit of dark purple, considered a delicacy, has several white fleshy segments inside with a sweet, sharp taste.

Longan – Thai longans, round thin-shelled fruits with a sweet pinkish-white flesh, are considered the best in the world.

Mango –Thailand is home to many varieties of mango, some of which can be eaten unripe, some either ripe or unripe. Sour mango is eaten with a sweet salty dip, while ripe mangoes are typically enjoyed with sticky rice.

Durian – this large spiky fruit, the 'King of Fruits' for many, is characterized by its pungent smell. Its flesh is noted for its subtle flavour and smooth texture.

Custard Apple – looking a bit like a hand grenade, this is a many-segmented fruit with lots of seeds.

Rose Apple – a bell-shaped fruit with a glossy pink or green skin that is eaten along with the crisp, slightly acid inside.

Jackfruit – shaped like a large melon, the fruit has a great number of large seeds and a yellow succulent flesh, odorous and tangy.

Young Coconut – both a beverage and a fruit with soft tender meat, an ideal refresher on a hot day.

Sapodilla – resembling a small brown mango, the fruit is eaten by removing the peel and slicing the reddish-brown flesh into pieces.

Andaman Coast

Moving to the peninsula further south, you discover a region more truly tropical, with higher rainfall imparting a deeper green to the natural vegetation and long palm-fringed beaches and islands bringing to life picture-postcard images of a tropical escape. Culturally, too, the region is distinct, stemming in part from a historical culture that developed far removed from Bangkok and partly from a strong Muslim influence in many areas.

On each side of the peninsula, the west facing the Andaman Sea and the east the Gulf of Thailand, are to be found the Kingdom's best known beach destinations, Phuket and Ko Samui, Thailand's largest and third largest islands respectively. Both loom large in tourism brochures and as such dominate their respective regions in the traveller's mind, though they are simply the biggest draws in what are multiple attractions.

Extending 48 km (30 miles) in length and 21 km (13 miles) at is widest point, Phuket encompasses scenic diversity in its widely different beach locales, urban centres and a hilly interior of both virgin forest and cultivated plantations. From being a backpackers' haven in the 1970s, Phuket has rocketed to tourism stardom, annually hosting more than three million visitors who flock to the superb beaches, luxury resort hotels and spas.

The island is no stranger to fame or wealth, however, and Phuket has long been on the map, known to early Arab and Indian seafarers and later, in the 16th and 17th centuries, to various Western explorers and traders. Then called Junkceylon, the island was renowned for its natural harbours, tin mines – and pirates.

In the 17th century, the French had their eyes on Junkceylon and its tin trade, but failed spectacularly to secure diplomatic relations with the Thais. A hundred years later Captain Francis Light hesitated whether to take Junkceylon or the Malay island of Penang for the British. He eventually plumped for the latter, thus saving Phuket from a colonial fate.

Quick to follow up on what the British had ignored were the Burmese who first attacked the island in 1785. They met greater resistance than they bargained for in the form of two sisters, Chan and Mook. These valiant ladies, so the chronicles have it, rallied the people of Junkceylon and broke the Burmese siege of the island. Today, at a crossroads in the centre of Phuket, you'll see a statue

of these heroines, brandishing swords and still keeping a wary eye out for invaders.

The Burmese attacked again in the early 19th century but although Chan and Mook were no longer manning the ramparts, success again eluded them. With peace came prosperity and, stimulated by a huge influx of Chinese immigrants adept at trade, tin mining boomed. Its legacy survives today in the form of several well-preserved Sino-Portuguese-style mansions that were originally built by the tin barons.

When tin mining went into decline in the latter part of the 20th century, tourism rose to take its place as the major money-spinner, so perpetuating the island's ranking as one of the country's wealthiest provinces. Prosperous though it was and remains, Phuket has always been renowned for its natural beauty rather than its wealth. In spite of substantial modern development, Phuket is a stunningly beautiful island. With a causeway linking it to the mainland, it hangs from Thailand's southern peninsula like an emerald pendant. Its interior is one of forested hills and valleys where the lush greens of rubber, coconut and pineapple plantations dapple the rich hues of natural tropical vegetation. The land drops to a rugged coastline on the east side, which stands in marked contrast to the gently sloping western shores, where a dozen sheltered bays harbour a string of white sandy beaches.

Above right: Increasingly Phuket is becoming a yachting haven as well as a destination for seekers of sun, sea and sand.

Opposite: The headland of Laem Phrom Thep, at the southern tip of Phuket, is a famed viewing point for watching the sunset.

VEGETARIAN FESTIVAL

A dramatic example of Chinese influence is Phuket's Vegetarian Festival held every year in October. This nine-day religious rite, marked by various rituals and parades in honour of the nine emperor gods, was first introduced at the turn of the century and is now celebrated at the island's five main Chinese temples.

Essentially an act of purification, the Vegetarian Festival is most spectacularly celebrated by acts of self-mortification, and you can witness the sight of devotees walking across beds of hot coals, piercing their cheeks with skewers, climbing knife-blade ladders and submitting themselves to other similar ordeals without apparent harm.

Overshadowed by its international reputation for sun, sea and sand, but nonetheless part of the attraction, is the island's intriguing cultural fabric. Over the centuries Phuket has been a melting pot and today offers a fascinating blend of Thai, Chinese and Muslim traditions. Differences are graphically witnessed in the juxtaposition of ornate Thai Buddhist temples, rather more garishly coloured Chinese temples and the minarets and domes of mosques. Yet the architectural contrasts belie an ethnic harmony for diverse influences have been comfortably absorbed. Although a complete vacation destination in itself, Phuket does not have a monopoly on magnificent sights and scenes in the area, and has proved a catalyst for opening up tourism in other nearby locations. Among these are the Similan island group, a renowned dive site, and Phang Nga Bay with its myriad weird and wonderfully shaped limestone outcrops.

On the mainland, Krabi has fewer beaches than Phuket, but challenges it in terms of natural beauty. Indeed, Krabi province as a whole, coast and hinterland, is characterized by karst outcrops, towering limestone cliffs that loom out of nowhere to create a landscape of rare natural grandeur. The rugged shore is studded with quiet coves sheltering soft, white sandy beaches backed by palm groves, while offshore islands, among them the twin Phi Phi islands, where much of the Hollywood movie *The Beach* was filmed, vie for attention.

Complementing blue sea and white sand is the lush green interior of Krabi province, highlighted at Khao Phanom Bencha National Park, a lush nature preserve covering some 50 km² (19 sq miles) of rainforest and noted for its impressive waterfalls, and Than Bokkharani National Park, an immensely picturesque area of limestone mountains, waterfalls, pools, mangrove forests, caves and islands.

South of Krabi, the province of Trang similarly blends coastal and inland beauty, albeit in a less spectacular fashion, and with far less fanfare. Offshore islands and inland caves and waterfalls are the province's main features, along with a less developed tourism infrastructure and hence greater local colour.

Last of the Andaman coast provinces, Satun is one of those quiet, peaceful places that most visitors overlook. So far with little tourism infrastructure, it nonetheless has most of the natural ingredients that make the Andaman coast so attractive to the traveller. Limestone outcrops rising out of a leafy green landscape are typical as, too, is the strong Muslim influence.

What really distinguishes Satun, however, is Tarutao National Marine Park. Established as Thailand's first marine environment preserve in 1974, Tarutao comprises 51 mountainous and forested islands, with caves, mangrove swamps and beaches strung along their shorelines. A comparatively isolated spot until modern times – it was a penal colony between 1939 and 1946 – Tarutao is as near pristine in its natural beauty as you'll find anywhere in the country.

Opposite above left: Featured in the movie *The Man with the Golden Gun*, this outcrop in Phang Nga Bay has become known as 'James Bond Island'.

Opposite above right: Outlying islands, such a Ko Poda in Krabi, beckon at many spots along the Andaman coast.

Opposite below: Ko Kradan and other islands off the coast of Trang are among the newer destinations to attract international visitors.

Above: Satun, the southernmost province on the Andaman coast, preserves in its relative isolation some superb natural scenery.

Right: Rubber trees were first introduced to Thailand in Trang and huge plantations remain a cornerstone of the local economy.

Opposite: A fishing boat's guardian spirit is believed to reside in the prow and it is honoured with brightly coloured ribbons.

Gulf of Thailand

On the opposite side of the southern peninsula, Ko Samui competes with Phuket as the country's top island in the sun. In many ways a classic resort, lending itself perfectly to travel-poster pictures of palm-shaded tropical beaches, Samui is an island apart, preserving an identity of its own.

Located in the Gulf of Thailand off the coast of Surat Thani province, Samui covers an area of 247 km² (95 sq miles). Roughly rectangular in shape, each of the four sides is defined by coastlines that present contrasting scenes, from long stretches of sand to quiet rocky coves, while the interior is made up of high rugged hills covered with the dense greenery of tropical forest and coconut plantations. Then there is the wider picture, which sets Samui as the largest among an archipelago of some 80 islands, the vast majority uninhabited and untouched by modern development.

In what has been effectively a separate history – the islanders still refer to themselves as *chao samui*, 'Samui people'. It was immigrants from the Chinese island of Hainan who first put Samui on the map when they settled there in the 19th century and began large-scale cultivation of the coconut palm. The business prospered to the extent that the island earned a reputation as the world's largest coconut plantation, and what appears today as a refreshingly green backdrop to the beaches was, until the tourism boom, the islanders' main source of livelihood.

With coconut farming and fishing offering a good living, nothing much disturbed Samui's traditional way of life and quiet air of independence until the late 1970s and early 1980s, when the island became fabled as a backpackers' paradise, the latest in a long list of legendary Asian dream worlds where the living is easy.

But once direct flights from Bangkok began in the mid 1980s, eliminating the tedious journey to Surat Thani and then a longish ferry ride, Samui started to appeal to the more well-heeled traveller and tourism infrastructure developed accordingly. Some backpackers remain, although the real diehards have moved to the nearby, more basic island of Ko Pha Ngan, famous – or infamous, depending on your view – for its full-moon beach parties.

As with all holiday resorts, the island has inevitably changed as it strives to cater to the mixed tastes of the international tourism market. Hotels, from budget to deluxe, restaurants, bars, shops and entertainment spots have all mushroomed in recent years. Some of the new infrastructure is undoubtedly regrettable, cheap and tawdry, although much is to be applauded and there are some deluxe hotels of true international excellence.

The island's most classically beautiful beach, a graceful 6-km (4-mile) sweep of white sand set between the blue of the sea and a green fringe of palms, is Chaweng, on Samui's east coast. It is also the island's most crowded and most developed beach. Natural beauty has not been totally obliterated – it is a stunning stretch of coastline – though the wealth of bungalows and hotels in all categories and the range of watersports on offer hamper an appreciation of the scenery and shatter any dream of a quiet escape. That said, there is plenty of space and, unlike the popular Mediterranean resorts, for example, the beach is not carpeted with bodies baking in the sun.

Behind Chaweng beach is a shift of scene. Here the road is lined with a near endless string of bars, cafes, discos, souvenir stalls, convenience stores, tattoo parlours and more. It is very much a young people's scene and a party atmosphere prevails.

Above left: Contrasting with the surrounding blue sea is Ko Samui's lush green interior of forest hills and coconut plantations.

Opposite above left: Old Samui can still be glimpsed in quiet streets of wooden shophouses and the local fondness for keeping caged song birds.

Opposite above right: Everything the budget traveller could wish for is to be found in the street behind Chaweng Beach.

Opposite below: A sense of the timelessness of island life is captured in the sight of a fisherman hauling in his net.

The next beach down the east coast, Lamai, is similar to Chaweng, only slightly shorter, almost as scenic, especially with the rock formations at the southern promontory, and equally developed to cater to a mass market. A tinseltown of bars, clubs and restaurants has similarly grown up behind the beach and, it must be admitted, Lamai and Chaweng are not everyone's idea of an idyllic escape to a tropical isle.

However, a little way down the east coast, the old Muslim fishing village at Ban Hua Thanon, with its fleet of colourfully painted southern Thai-style fishing boats, seems miles from Lamai, although it is located just around the headland, and as you travel around the island's southern coast tourism development becomes conspicuously less evident. The beaches here in no way compare to the long sandy strands of Chaweng and Lamai, being much smaller, shallower and tending to dry out at low tide, but they possess a

different sort of beauty in tranquil ,coconut-grove-shaded coves and typical old fishing villages.

The scene shifts again on the western side of the island, which, although more developed than the southern shore, is still placid. If the beaches here are not the best, considerable compensation can be found in some splendid headlands and in pretty bays. Further up the coast the beaches and scenery are flatter and less attractive, that is until late afternoon when there is plenty to captivate the imagination in the sunsets that are often magnificent.

Samui's west side also boasts its capital, Nathon, which was the island's biggest commercial centre until the latter-day build-up behind Chaweng and Lamai beaches. Today, Nathon has the air of a service station and transport centre, and to get closest to the Samui of old, it's best to visit the northern coast, which, if not devoid of development, retains more of an old-world atmosphere

BIG BUDDHA

Located on Ko Samui's northeast cape is the 'Big Buddha' at Wat Phra Yai. Prosaically – if aptly – named this is Samui's only real monumental attraction, a huge 12-m (39-ft) high golden image of the sitting Buddha that, sited on a small rocky islet reached by a causeway, dominates the shoreline for miles around.

Wat Phra Yai is not strictly speaking a temple, being without the characteristic preaching and ordination halls, but rather it is a shrine, erected in 1972 as place on the island where visitors, all Thais at that time, could make merit. Today, people from all over the world flock to this famous landmark.

in a few remaining old wooden houses and traditional two-storey seafront shophouses.

With Samui's diversity of attractions and wealth of natural beauty, it is easy to forget that it is part of an archipelago and that there are other islands to explore. Popular with backpackers is Ko Pha Ngan, a short boat ride to the north, while further away is Ko Tao, one of the country's best dive spots.

Of all the islands, however, it is those in Ang Thong Marine National Park that score highest for sheer beauty and excursion potential. Located 31 km (19 miles) west of Samui, the park covers more than 100 km² (39 sq miles) and comprises a group of some 40 lovely steep-sided limestone islands fringed with forest. The shore is lined with coves and limestone caves, while the lush interior is home to a wealth of flora and fauna from rare orchids to a dazzling variety of monkeys and birds.

Above left: Ko Samui is not all sun, sea and sand, and the island's interior offers a number of scenic spots such as Na Muang Waterfall.

Opposite: Workhorses they may be, but the boats of southern Thai fishing communities are typically brightly painted and decorated.

The Far South

Thai Muslims, the country's largest religious minority, mostly inhabit the country's southernmost provinces. Here long ago were prosperous and independent kingdoms, though today, while traditions remain deep-rooted, little architectural evidence survives to signpost the past. Moreover, a relative lack of modern development has caused friction, especially in the three most southerly provinces of Yala, Patani and Narathiwat, where sporadic and comparatively low-key insurgency has deterred tourism.

Away from the trouble spots, the provincial capital of Nakhon Si Thammarat and the beach resort of Songkhla tend to be overlooked by most visitors, yet both are rewarding destinations in their own different ways.

Nakhon Si Thammarat has an extraordinarily rich past and has played a key role in the religious and cultural development of Thailand, but while the heydays are long gone and the city now features more prominently in history books than in guidebooks, it's a mistake to write the place off as merely a has-been. If it lacks any obvious urban charm, it is possessed of an air of quiet self-confidence that speaks of the importance of its heritage as a religious and trading centre dating back to the early centuries AD.

Today's visitor finds a glorious reminder of Nakhon Si Thammarat's religious importance in Wat Phra Mahathat, the most sacred Buddhist shrine in southern Thailand and one of the most fascinating temples in the entire country. Its age is uncertain and while historians date its founding to at least 1000 years ago, legend has it that the Buddha relic enshrined in its *chedi* was washed ashore after a shipwreck in the 4th century of the Buddhist era.

But Wat Phra Mahathat needs no legend to grab the attention; it is in every respect a superb and intriguing temple, its unusual architecture and decorative detail putting it in a class of its own. Surrounded by cloisters roofed with orange and green tiles, it is dominated by a magnificent Sri Lankan-style *chedi*, its massive base shaped like an overturned alms bowl and surmounted by a slender, graceful 77-m (253-ft) high spire tipped with gold.

Equally impressive is the complex of chapels around the base of the *chedi* within a compound studded with maze-like rows of smaller *chedis*. It is not only that the eye is caught at every turn by the intricacy of the architectural design, it is positively dazzled by the richly decorated interiors.

Travelling south from Nakhon Si Thammarat, past the huge Thale Sap Songkhla inland sea, an important reserve for waterfowl, is Hat Yai, the biggest city in the far south. This is an important business and commercial hub, but otherwise unremarkable – memorably described as 'reminiscent of Bangkok without the interesting bits'. Just some 25 km (16 miles) away, however, is the coastal resort of Songkhla.

Quiet and unpretentious in spite of a long history, Songhkla has a restful ambience and charm all its own. With sufficient architectural and historical sights to sustain interest, along with the long, casuarina-fringed Samila Beach, it's an ideal spot for a relaxing escape away from it all.

Above: Wat Phra Mahathat is Nakhon Si Thammarat's most famous sight and one of the most intriguing temples in the entire country.

Opposite above: A bronze mermaid wringing water from her hair at the far end of Songkhla's Samila beach pays tribute to the earth goddess Thorani.

NANG TALUNG

Traditional to Thailand's far south, *Nang Talung* is a type of shadow theatre staged with cut-out buffalo-hide figures that have movable arms, legs and chin manipulated by a concealed puppeteer.

Stories usually take their theme from daily life and are typically improvised by the puppeteer who accompanies the performance with dialogue and songs. *Nang Talung* is now all but extinct, but an insight into this once popular form of entertainment can be glimpsed at the Shadow Puppet Workshop, a private puppet theatre and museum in Nakhon Si Thammarat.

Above: Walking the pristine sands of Ko Poda off the coast of Krabi is a blissful alternative to the more crowded beaches of the mainland.

Left: Any of the numerous uninhabited islands in the Andaman Sea more than lives up to anyone's dream of a tropical island escape.

Opposite: Maya Beach on Ko Phi Phi was chosen as the location for the ultimate backpacker's quest in the Hollywood movie *The Beach*.

Chapter Four

Historical Heartland

The Central Plains

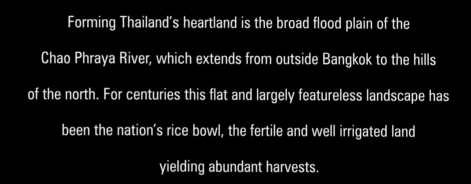

Forming Thailand's heartland is the broad flood plain of the

Chao Phraya River, which extends from outside Bangkok to the hills

of the north. For centuries this flat and largely featureless landscape has

been the nation's rice bowl, the fertile and well irrigated land

yielding abundant harvests.

Opposite above left: Broad and well watered, the rural areas of the fertile Central Plains form a patchwork of paddy fields.

Above left: Mechanical harvesters are comparatively rare and gathering the rice crop is more commonly a labour-intensive and back-breaking human task.

Opposite left: The huge seated Buddha image enshrined at Wat Phanan Choeng in Ayutthaya is especially revered by Thais of Chinese descent.

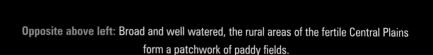

Left: Architectural detail of Wat Phra Si Ratana Mahathat in Lopburi, which dates back to Khmer times but was restored and enlarged in the 17th century.

Historical Heartland

"Within the walls were some of the most magnificent buildings to be seen in the Orient – including three major palace complexes..."

It is also here that the Thais established their first capital, Sukhothai, on the northern edge of the plains, which was later superseded by Ayutthaya, on the Chao Phraya at the lower edge of the flatlands. It is this historical importance of the region that today holds the greatest attraction for the visitor, beginning with Ayutthaya, which is popularly toured on a day trip from Bangkok.

Ayutthaya

Situated some 85 km (53 miles) north of Bangkok, Ayutthaya thrives today, but only as a country town and the prevailing atmosphere is a far cry from the regal splendour, pageantry and cosmopolitan air than once pervaded the site. Nevertheless, there are sufficient ruins, now preserved as a UNESCO World Heritage Site, to capture the imagination.

Occupying an island formed by the junction of the Chao Phraya, Pa Sak and Lopburi rivers, Ayutthaya is estimated to have housed a population of one million inhabitants at the height of its power, and comprised a walled city 12 km (7.5 miles) in circumference and criss-crossed by a 140-km (87-mile) network of canals. Within the walls were some of the most magnificent buildings to be seen in the Orient – including three major palace complexes and some 400 temples. There were also clearly defined quarters for soldiers, scholars, artists and artisans who contributed to the glory and well-being of the city, as well as the 'factories' of the Oriental and European nations that conducted a thriving trade with Ayutthaya.

The totality of old Ayutthaya is hard to imagine today and can only really be pictured by drawing comparisons with Bangkok. As with Bangkok, sightseeing is best begun at the old royal city. Little of Ayutthaya's royal palace survives except for its foundations, but the former royal temple, Wat Phra Si Sanphet, remains a most impressive and imposing ruin.

The equivalent of Bangkok's Temple of the Emerald Buddha, Wat Phra Si Sanphet dates from the 14th century and today is most famous for its three aligned *chedis* that epitomise classic Ayutthaya-style religious architecture. Originally, however, Wat Phra Si Sanphet was remarkable for enshrining a 'prodigious colossus', as the 17th-

century Jesuit Guy Tachard described the temple's presiding image, a 16-m (52-ft) tall bronze statue of the standing Buddha. Not only was this the largest standing image ever cast, it was also covered with more than 170 kg (375 lb) of gold leaf.

Above: Mischievous monkeys roam over the ancient Khmer ruins of Wat Phra Sam Yot located in the heart of Lopburi.

Opposite above left: Dating from the mid-14th century, Ayutthaya's Wat Yai Chai Mongkol was formerly a famous mediation centre.

Opposite above right: Bird life is rich throughout Thailand. These Asian open billed storks were spotted in a paddy field in the Central Plains.

Opposite below: Founded in 1369 but restored in the 15th century, Wat Phra Ram in Ayutthaya is unmistakable for its finely proportioned *prang*.

BANG PA-IN

An arresting little sight 20 km (12 miles) downstream from Ayutthaya, Bang Pa-In is a former royal summer retreat comprising a collection of bijou regal buildings set amid formal gardens adorned with European statuary. First developed by the kings of Ayutthaya in the 17th century, the present constructions date from the late 19th and early 20th centuries. The complex is attractively laid out and displays a surprising variety of architectural styles, including Thai, Chinese, Italian and Victorian.

Most charming of all are the ornate Thai-style Aisawan Tippaya Asna pavilion (right) sited in the middle of an ornamental lake, and Wat Niwet Tham Prawat, a Buddhist chapel curiously designed in the style of a neo-Gothic church.

For present-day visitors, a good idea of just how imposing this image was is afforded by the adjacent modern temple of Wat Mongkhon Bophit, which enshrines a smaller, but still huge, 15th-century bronze image of the seated Buddha. For an appreciation of the scale and complexity of Wat Phra Si Sanphet and the entire former royal complex, there is a detailed model in the Ayutthaya Historical Study Centre.

Wat Phra Si Sanphet stands at the western end of the main east-west axis that was the heart of ancient Ayutthaya, dividing the royal city to the north from the commercial area to the south. Here, a number of major monuments are within easy walking distance, among them the splendid Wat Ratchaburana.

In a comparatively good state of preservation, the temple was built in 1424 by King Borommaracha II on the cremation site of his two elder brothers who died while fighting each other on elephant back over the rights to the throne. At the front of the site loom the high brick walls of an ordination hall 63 m (207 ft) long by 20 m (66 ft) wide, but the focus of attention is the massive central tower that has been well restored with parts of it stucco decoration intact.

It was at Wat Ratchaburana that one of the most important archaeological finds of the modern era was made when, in 1957, the crypt of the tower was excavated and revealed traces of mural paintings along with a valuable stash of jewellery and other gold objects which are now on show at the Chao Sam Phraya National Museum. The interior of the tower remains accessible and to descend the precipitous stone stairs gives an inkling of the thrill of archaeological discovery.

Below: One of Ayutthaya's best-known temple ruins, Wat Ratchaburana was constructed in1424 on the site where two princes had killed one another during a duel on elephant-back.

Across the road from Wat Ratchaburana are the extensive ruins of Wat Mahathat, once the residence of the City Patriarch. The site is dominated by the base of a huge *prang* that formerly rose to a height of 46 m (151 ft), although more memorable is the sight of a Buddha head that has become entwined among tree roots to produce a haunting image of the passage of time and nature's ultimate dominance.

Many sights are scattered beyond the central core, among the most worthwhile being Wat Yai Chai Mongkol, located to the southeast, across the Pa Sak river. The monastery, which still supports a religious community, was originally built in 1357 and is distinguished by its *chedi* constructed to commemorate King Naresuan's victory in single-handed combat on elephant back over the Crown Prince of Burma in 1592.

Non-religious sights include the kraal where the king's war elephants were stabled, and the remains of the former Portuguese and Japanese settlements. These may lack the visual interest of the temple ruins, but they do offer insights into important facets of life during the Ayutthaya period.

No tour of Ayutthaya would be complete without some travel by boat, which enhances an impression of the island setting and parallels the way early travellers would have first encountered the city. Downstream on the Pa Sak, close to its junction with the Chao Phraya, stands Wat Phanan Choeng. Believed to pre-date the founding of Ayutthaya by some 26 years, the temple is noted for its huge image of the seated Buddha, dating from 1324. Westward, up the Chao Phraya, lies the restored Wat Phuthai-Sawan, constructed in 1353 by the banks of the river on the site of the former residence of Prince U Thong. Its central *prang* and smaller *chedis* provide a sharp contrast to the nearby European form of St. Joseph's Cathedral, a latter-day reconstruction of an original Portuguese church.

Finally, at the bend in the river is the 17th-century Wat Chai Wattanaram, arguably the most imposing of all Ayutthaya's monuments, partly because of its size and architectural sophistication, but also for its tranquil riverside setting well away from the bustle of the modern town.

Above right: A statue of the reclining Buddha at Wat Phuthai-Sawan, built in 1353 on the site of the residence of Ayutthaya's founder, Prince U Thong.

Right: A stone Buddha head entwined in the roots of a tree at Ayutthaya's Wat Mahathat is a poignant reminder of the passage of time.

Opposite: The tall *chedi* of Wat Yai Chai Mongkol, Ayutthaya, commemorates King Naresuan's victory over the Burmese in 1592.

Above: Once the royal chapel, Wat Phra Si Sanphet, highlighted by its three aligned *chedis*, attests to Ayutthaya's former splendour.

Right: Dating from 1491, Wat Phra Si Sanphet stands inside what was originally the compound of Ayutthaya's royal palace.

Opposite: Although a comparatively late Ayutthaya temple, Wat Chai Wattanaram is remarkable for both its superb and imposing architecture and its picturesque riverside location.

Lopburi

History continues to unfold at Lopburi, north of Ayutthaya on the banks of the river of the same name. Admittedly, it is not at first glance an interesting town, but a little judicious sightseeing reveals amid the modern concrete sprawl a number of ancient ruins that are clear indications that the town has seen better days.

From earliest times, Lopburi was a place of some note. Archaeological evidence suggests the area supported organized habitation in the prehistoric era and traces of a New Stone Age culture have been unearthed. Later, between the 7th and 11th centuries, the town was a major centre of the Dvaravati (Mon) kingdom.

During the 10th to late 13th centuries Lopburi was an important outpost of the Khmer empire, ruled at one time by a Khmer viceroy. The legacy of this period is seen in a handful of ruined temples, the most important being Phra Prang Sam Yot, a splendid monument to the Bayon style in spite of today standing slap in the centre of town and being hideously bounded on one side by railway tracks.

Lopburi's single most imposing religious ruin, however, is Wat Phra Si Ratana Mahathat. It is situated opposite the railway station in yet another example of the modern town's uncanny habit of blending the venerable with the mean. It is an extensive site dominated by a large laterite Khmer *prang*, though the temple is most fascinating for its overall construction which spans the Khmer period and the 17th century. Most likely first erected in the 12th century and remodelled in the 14th, it was later considerably expanded by King Narai (ruled 1656–88), a process witnessed by the large brick *viharn*.

Indeed, if Lopburi belongs historically to anyone, it is properly the domain of King Narai, who made the city his second capital when he elected to move his court there for part of each year, turning the city into a sort of Versailles to Ayutthaya's Paris. The move was

partly defensive, and partly due to Lopburi's surroundings that were rich in wild elephant herds, the hunting of the beast being a favourite pastime of the monarch.

The parallel with Versailles was given some substance when, in the 1680s, Narai received two embassies from France's King Louis XIV, hosting them at both Ayutthaya and Lopburi. It was the hope of the Thai monarch that he might achieve a mutually beneficial alliance with France; however, his plans were thwarted by conservative courtiers who feared the French wished to convert Narai to Catholicism. Matters were brought to an abrupt end when, as the king lay on his death bed, a court revolution in 1688 brought about the expulsion of the French, along with most other foreigners, effectively closing the door on international relations for the next 200 years. In many respects King Narai was ahead of his time and not until the 1850s did Thailand look again to the West.

Above: Phaulkon's House in Lopburi was both the residence of King Narai's Greek advisor and a place used to host visiting foreign embassies.

Right: Solidly constructed out of stone, this Western-style chapel in the compound of Phaulkon's House was built for foreign envoys.

Opposite above left: Combining the mundane with the sublime, present-day Lopburi encompasses a surprising number of venerable monuments.

Opposite above right: Honoured with this statue in the royal palace, King Narai made Lopburi his second capital, a welcome retreat from the complicated intrigues of Ayutthaya.

France had failed in her 17th century attempt at establishing political and commercial links with Thailand, but she had made a lasting impact in other respects. Lopburi was left with an indelible Gallic stamp.

Firstly there are the ruins of Narai's palace, a grandiose affair that was partially designed by French architects and consisting of courtyards set within courtyards, the whole surrounded by huge crenellated walls pierced at intervals by tall, imposing gateways. What little remains of the interior buildings is mostly in ruins, but the walls and gates are as imposing as ever.

Not far away is Phaulkon's House, also known as the 'Ambassadors' Residence' as French delegates stayed there. It again shows a strong European influence in design. Only the exterior walls have survived, but the architectural borrowings are clear, while the use of stone attests to the importance of the building.

FALCON OF SIAM

The most influential man at the court of Siam during the last years of King Narai was not a Thai but a Greek, Constantine Phaulkon, his surname being an Anglicized version of the *Greek Gerákis*, meaning 'falcon'. Perhaps the most amazing foreigner ever to play a role in Thai politics, Phaulkon was born on the island of Cephalonia in 1647 and as a boy ran away to sea, serving on trading ships of the English East India Company.

After surviving shipwrecks and various other adventures, he arrived in Ayutthaya in 1678, where his considerable charm, talent for intrigue, and gift for languages brought him to the attention of King Narai, who appointed him his minister for trade, which at the time meant effectively foreign minister. As the King's foreign adviser, and indeed favourite, Phaulkon played a key role in negotiations with the French embassies of 1685 and 1687, walking a diplomatic tightrope in trying to win French support for Narai's political aims while, at the same time, appeasing conservative elements at court wary of a growing foreign presence. He was doomed to failure.

During his rise to power, Phaulkon had made numerous enemies, partly through his own arrogance and partly through others' envy of his wealth and position. In 1688, Phaulkon was arrested during a palace revolution led by General Petracha. He was charged with treason and, without the protection of his ailing benefactor, was imprisoned, tortured and finally executed.

Pictured above are the ruins of Phaulkon's grand residence in Lopburi.

Right: Wat Phra Sam Yot, in the centre of Lopburi, dates back to the 13th century when the town was an important outpost of the Khmer empire.

DEATH RAILWAY

As part of its war strategy to conquer Burma (as Myanmar was then called), the Japanese forced Allied PoWs, as well as Thai and other Asian labourers, to build a 415-km (258-mile) railway between Thailand and Burma. A vital link in this supply line was a bridge to span the River Kwai Yai in Thailand's Kanchanaburi province.

Engineers estimated that it would take five years to build the railway – the Japanese army had it completed in 16 months at the cost of the lives of 16,000 British, Dutch, Australian, American, Malay and Indian PoWs and an estimated 100,000 Thai and other Asian forced labourers, who died from inhumane treatment, malnutrition and disease.

The line was in use for 20 months before the Allies bombed and partially destroyed the River Kwai bridge in 1945.

Western Thailand

The corner of Thailand lying west of Bangkok is not strictly a part of the Central Plains, lying on the edge of the lowlands and extending into the mountains that form the border between Thailand and Myanmar, But, like Ayutthaya, it is generally visited as a day trip from the Thai capital.

Immediately west of Bangkok is Nakhon Pathom, one of the country's oldest settlements and site of what was a Mon capital during the Dvaravati period (6th–11th century) and the earliest known centre of Buddhist learning in Thailand. The present town is dominated by the Phra Pathom Chedi, the world's tallest Buddhist monument, which marks the location of an ancient *chedi* that was destroyed in the 11th century.

Further west, modern history is vividly recalled at Kanchanaburi, site of the infamous Bridge over the River Kwai which was constructed by allied POWs of the Japanese during the Second World War. It is not as impressive as you might expect, but the town's two impeccably kept war cemeteries give a moving reminder of one of the war's darkest episodes.

Contrasting with tragic history is the natural beauty of Kanchanaburi province, an area in which jungle-clad hills, wooded river valleys, caves and waterfalls offer some of the most picturesque scenery to be found anywhere in Thailand.

Right: The Kanchanaburi countryside is possessed of extraordinary natural charm, Erawan Falls being one of the most popular beauty spots.

Sukhothai

Writing about Sukhothai in the 1920s, English forestry official Reginald Campbell remarked, 'For all the desolate, miserable, god-forsaken places on this earth, Sukhothai must surely be the worst.'

Located on the northern edge of the Central Plains, 450 km (280 miles) from Bangkok, present-day Sukhothai is perhaps not one of Thailand's most inspiring towns, but just 12 km (7.5 miles) away are the magnificent ruins of the Kingdom's first capital, founded in c.1240, from which the modern town takes its name.

Mr Campbell may have had a blind spot for the history of his host country, though his complete silence regarding the historical remains of Sukhothai is indicative of the neglect the ancient site suffered until comparatively recently.

In Campbell's day the ruins were probably all but obscured by jungle. Today's traveller is more fortunate. Following the completion in 1988 of a 10-year UNESCO restoration project and its subsequent designation as a World Heritage Site, Sukhothai now beckons as a fascinating historical park. Full former glory is beyond retrieval, but the ruins that remain mark the cultural centre of Thailand and recall the early flowering of Thai civilization.

Within the confines of the ancient city's ramparts are more than 20 major monuments, while numerous other sights are scattered throughout the impeccably maintained park which covers a total area of 70 km² (27 sq miles). Any tour is best started at the Ramkhamhaeng National Museum, where a good collection of sculpture and other artifacts affords the visitor a useful introduction to the period.

From the museum it is just a few steps to the heart of the ancient city and Wat Mahathat. This is the biggest and most magnificent of Sukhothai's temples and is dominated by a *chedi* in the form of a lotus bud, a design unique to Sukhothai-period architecture. On the surrounding platform are four *stupas* and four *prangs*, while the base is decorated with stucco figures of Buddhist disciples. To the sides are two giant statues of the standing Buddha, and on the eastern side are twin rows of pillars and a platform with a large image of the seated Buddha.

This is a classic Sukhothai monument while close by Khmer influences can be seen in Wat Sri Sawai. Comprising three large *prangs*, it probably pre-dates the founding of the Thai capital and may have first been built as a shrine to the Hindu god Shiva before being converted to Buddhist use.

Also of note in this central area are the ruins of Wat Trapang Ngoen, picturesquely sited on an island in the middle of an ornamental lake, and Wat Sra Sri which has a fine typically rounded *chedi* in Sri Lankan style.

Above: Dwarfed by the statue, a man applies gold leaf to the huge Buddha image at Sukhothai's Wat Si Chum in an act of devotion.

Opposite: The former magnificence of Sukhothai is wonderfully evoked by the lotus-bud *chedi*, Buddha images and temple columns of Wat Mahathat.

LOY KRATHONG

Most enchanting of all Thailand's annual festivals, Loy Krathong, which celebrates the end of the rainy season on the night of the November full moon, is popularly believed to have originated in its present form at Sukhothai. According to legend, there was at the royal court of King Ramkhamhaeng (ruled c.1279–1298) a beautiful young lady named Nang Nopphamas, the daughter of a Brahmin priest. One year, in the 12th lunar month, she witnessed the king and his courtiers picnicking by boat on the city's canals as part of the celebration of Mae Khongkha, 'Mother of Waters'.

However, with her knowledge of Brahmin rituals, she felt the Thai ceremony lacked a certain touch of beauty and enchantment. Thus, with great skill Nang Nopphamas crafted a krathong, a small 'boat' fashioned out of banana leaves in the shape of a lotus flower. After lighting candles and incense, she floated (loy in Thai) this charming gift towards the King who graciously accepted it. And so was born the symbol that has ever since marked the celebration of Loy Krathong.

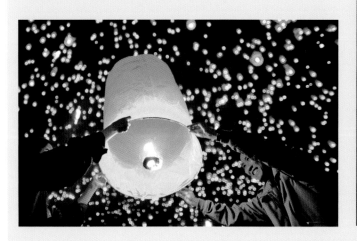

Of the several monuments located outside the old city walls, two are not to be missed. Wat Phra Phai Luang, lying about a 10-minute walk beyond the northern gateway, is an extensive ruin that rivals Wat Mahathat in importance. Its Khmer-style *prang* predates the Thai period and, in all, three separate stages of construction can be discerned as the once Hindu shrine was converted to a Buddhist temple. In front of the *prang* are the ruins of a *viharn* and a *chedi*, the base of the latter being decorated with stucco Buddha images. Nearby is a *mondop* enclosing the ruined statues of the Buddha in walking, standing, sitting and reclining postures.

Southwest of Wat Phra Phai Luang, Wat Si Chum is impressive for its huge *mondop* built around an enormous stucco-over-brick statue of the seated Buddha, measuring 11.3 m (37 ft) across the lap. Inside the walls of the *mondop* is a narrow passage where the ceiling is decorated with beautifully engraved stone slabs illustrating scenes from the Jataka tales which relate the previous incarnations of the Buddha.

Sukhothai was the principal city of the first Thai kingdom, but two other sites relatively close by add to one's appreciation of the achievement of the first Thai state.

From Sukhothai it is just 56 km (35 miles) north to the period's second city, Si Satchanalai, which, while much smaller, offers in its compact and picturesque setting a dimension of the past that can no longer be grasped from its more illustrious neighbour.

Nowhere is the power and majesty of Si Satchanalai more strongly expressed than in Wat Chang Lom. Located in the heart of the city but standing slightly apart from the other ruins, this is the site's most imposing monument. Some columns of the ruined *viharn* survive, but it is the large bell-shaped *chedi* that grabs the attention. It stands on a square base decorated with 39 elephant (*chang*) buttresses, many of which are today sadly disfigured. Also of note are the niches on the upper tier of the base, some still enshrining Buddha images.

Above right: Wat Phra Phai Luang, dominated by a Khmer-style *prang*, rivalled Sukhothai's Wat Mahathat in size and importance.

Right: The massive Buddha image at Wat Si Chum illustrates characteristic features of Sukhothai-era sculpture, such as the significantly extended ear lobes and a flame halo.

To the south, opposite Wat Chang Lom, are the extensive ruins of Wat Chedi Chet Thaew which occupies a large area and comprises seven (*chet*) rows of *chedis*. The latter were probably constructed to contain the ashes of members of the Sukhothai dynasty who ruled the city. Tapering up from a square base, the *chedis* display fragments of their original stucco decoration. In particular, the side of the central structure facing Wat Chang Lom has a fine stucco Buddha seated on a *naga* which is comparatively well preserved.

Next, closely sited in a line running southeast, are the ruins of Wat Uthayan Yai and Wat Nang Phaya. The western wall of the latter's *viharn* has some partly intact stucco decoration dating from the Ayutthaya period.

The third of the three major Sukhothai-period sites, Kamphaeng Phet, located some 75 km (47 miles) south of Sukhothai itself, today masks its ancient origins, having been swallowed up by a modern provincial town. As an inhabited site, however, it predates Sukhothai but only rose to a position of prominence in the latter half of the 14th century.

The name Kamphaeng Phet translates as 'Diamond Walls', and the city was originally a garrison town serving as a buffer between Sukhothai and the increasingly powerful younger city-state of Ayutthaya. The defences, as the name suggests, were considered impenetrable, although it was here that Sukhothai eventually submitted to Ayutthaya in 1378. But while the first Thai kingdom was eclipsed, Kamphaeng Phet retained its strategic value as a defensive point on Ayutthaya's northern frontier, as illustrated by the scattered remains of several fortresses dating from the 15th and 16th centuries.

Kamphaeng Phet's principal monuments fall into two groups: those situated inside the old city walls, abutting the edge of the modern town centre, and those remains lying in the wooded area on the northern outskirts. Of the former, the finest and most famous ruins are those of Wat Phra Kaeo. This was originally the city's royal temple and, as the name indicates, it once temporarily housed the Emerald Buddha statue, the nation's most sacred image now enshrined in Bangkok's temple of the same name. Built in the Sukhothai period and later restored by Ayutthayan architects, the laterite temple is dominated by a large *chedi*, raised on a high square base and ringed by a series of niches that were formerly adorned with lion statues.

Impressive though the architecture is, it is the Buddha statuary which catches the eye of today's visitor. The laterite images, worn away to evocative, almost abstract, shadows, possess an unusual charm, while a restored group of two seated Buddhas and a reclining image in brick and stucco expresses, notably in the faces, a splendid sense of serenity.

SUKHOTHAI ART

Buddha images of the Sukhothai period were far more stylized than anything that had gone before and are marked by a greater fluidity in the line of the body and an uncanny degree of serenity and spirituality expressed in the facial features.

Statues in the seated posture were popular, but the real triumph of the Sukhothai artists was the depiction of the walking Buddha. This posture had appeared before but only in carved relief and it was a Thai innovation to produce walking images in the round. But not only was originality achieved, it was accomplished in a most stunning fashion with the artists brilliantly capturing their subject in a frozen moment of movement.

Directly southeast of Wat Phra Kaeo is Wat Phra That, comprising an imposing collection of laterite columns and small *stupas* surrounding a large central *chedi*. The bell-shaped form of the latter is characteristic of the Sri Lankan style of Buddhist architecture, and attests to Sukhothai's influence during Kamphaeng Phet's golden age. Outside the original city walls, are some of Kamphaeng Phet's most atmospheric ruins – Wat Phra Non, with fragments of an enormous reclining Buddha, and Wat Phra Si Iriyabot, where giant restored images of the walking and standing Buddhas loom against brick alcoves.

Last of the major monuments is Wat Chang Rob, set apart from the other ruins about 1 km (1100 yd) to the north. The site was once dominated by a bell-shaped *chedi* of which only the base and lower levels can be seen today. Like similar monuments at Sukhothai and Si Satchanalai, it is notable for the 68 elephant buttresses that encircle the base, some of which, along with other stucco decorative detail, are still in comparatively good condition.

Small though it may be, Kamphaeng Phet is a fascinating complement to Sukhothai and Si Satchanalai, adding yet more to an appreciation of the glory that once was Sukhothai.

Opposite above: Buddha images at Wat Phra Kaeo in Kamphaeng Phet, arguably the most enchanting of the three main Sukhothai-era sites.

Right: An exquisite monument in every respect, Wat Chang Lom is the most wondrous of Si Satchanalai's temple ruins.

Chapter Five

Into the Hills

Chiang Mai and Northern Thailand

Although less than an hour's flight from the capital, northern Thailand is a land apart, with its own history and a distinct culture. Here are ancient towns, founded long before Bangkok and here, too, are rugged landscapes so different from the neat, level, patchwork fields of the Central Plains.

Opposite above left: Elephant buttresses surround the base of the 14th-century *chedi* at Wat Phra That Chang Kham in Nan.

Above left: The summit of Doi Mae Salong offers a panoramic view of Chiang Rai's remote and rugged hill country.

Opposite left: The rice harvest is a scene as characteristic of the northern countryside as it is elsewhere throughout Thailand.

Left: Fine hand-woven cotton on display in Nan where local textiles are among the region's top shopping attractions.

Into the Hills

"A clear sense of northern identity, rooted in a separate history ... is apparent in a people proud of their own heritage."

Topographically, the north is distinguished as an area of forested highlands traversed by parallel river valleys. The region boasts the country's highest peak, Doi Inthanon, along with other upland ranges that present picturesque, and in parts comparatively remote, landscapes. This is also teak country where work elephants once played an important role in the extraction of logs. Today, logging has been banned in an attempt to halt deforestation, although elephants remain characteristic features in the landscape and find new employment in providing tourist treks into the hills.

It is not only geography, however, that distinguishes the north; history, cultural traditions and ethnic make-up all contribute to a distinct identity. From the late 13th century until the early 1900s the region was largely independent, in its early heyday a thriving kingdom known as Lanna, 'the land of a million rice fields'. Autonomous development, coupled with strong influences from neighbouring Laos and Myanmar, resulted in distinctive northern arts and architecture.

A clear sense of northern identity, rooted in a separate history and supported by agricultural prosperity, is apparent in a people proud of their own heritage. Northerners tend to remain more faithful to long-held values than their Bangkok counterparts and are generally home-loving, thrifty and wary of spending money ostentatiously. The custom of entering the monkhood is still widespread among boys and young men, and ordination ceremonies are particularly elaborate and festive affairs.

Most of all, that quintessential Thai trait, *sanuk*, having a good time, thrives in the north where festivals are celebrated with greater panache and exuberance than elsewhere in the country, and where the local cuisine, with a strong Burmese influence, is a particular treat even in a land renowned for its culinary arts.

Left: Chiang Dao, Thailand's third highest peak at 2285 m (7500 ft), is a spectacular and awe-inspiring feature of the northern landscape.

Opposite above left: A view of the Kok River flowing past forested hills at Tha Ton, north of Chiang Mai.

Opposite above right: The mountain scenery of Chiang Rai, in the far north, appears wild and rugged, although it is surprisingly accessible.

Opposite below: Chiang Rai is the terminus for popular cruises by longtail boat down the Kok River from Tha Ton.

Chiang Mai

The heart of the northern hill country is Chiang Mai, established in the late 13th century as the capital of the Lanna kingdom and today Thailand's second city, not in size but in importance nationally and as a tourism hub. Growing apace over the last couple of decades – significantly several top luxury hotels have opened in the last few years – the city is no longer the quiet backwater it was when popularly known as 'The Rose of the North'. Yet it has taken on a contemporary mantle without shedding its individuality. It's also much more relaxed than Bangkok.

Drawing distinction from its location in a scenic valley and from the Ping River that flows through town, Chiang Mai keeps history alive in the square moat, city gates and walls of its old central core. Although these structures are reconstructions dating only from the 19th century and later, they embody a manifest sense of history and a cherished pride in the past.

Similarly, the city's handicraft heritage is proudly maintained, and in addition to traditional crafts there is now a vibrant contemporary interior design industry that attracts buyers from around the world. Woodcarving, silverware, pottery, lacquerware, weaving and, emblematic of Chiang Mai, paper umbrellas are all produced in artists' enclaves in and around the city. To stroll the streets, wander around the famed Night Bazaar, and search out the many excellent specialist shops and boutiques is to discover a treasure trove of quality crafts in both traditional and contemporary styles.

During its heyday, from the late 13th to the mid-16th centuries, Chiang Mai was an important centre of Theravada Buddhism (hosting the Eighth Buddhist World Council in 1455) and rivals Bangkok in its wealth of religious architecture. It is not more of the same, however, as Chiang Mai's temples are both older and stylistically different from those in the capital, most noticeably in their carved wooden pediments.

The largest of Chiang Mai's temples, Wat Phra Singh, was founded in 1345, although the imposing *viharn* that dominates the compound dates from 1925 and most merit lies in the older, smaller Viharn Laikam, which many consider the finest example of late-Lanna architecture still surviving in Chiang Mai. Enshrined here is the revered and venerable image of Phra Buddha Singh, while the interior has some excellent 19th-century mural paintings.

Striking in a very different way is Wat Chedi Luang. Here the temple buildings are comparatively modern and instead the attention is drawn to the huge ruined *chedi*. Built in 1401 and later enlarged to a height of 90 m (295 ft), the structure was damaged by an earthquake in 1545 and never restored. Nonetheless, what remains is impressive, and aside from the *chedi* itself, the compound also houses the City Pillar set beneath a gum tree that is believed to mark the spot where King Mengrai was killed by lightning in 1317.

SONGKRAN

All Thais love a festival but none celebrate with greater exuberance than northern Thais, which makes Chiang Mai one of the best spots to enjoy Songkran, the Thai New Year.

A nationwide festival, Songkran falls on 13th April, with the following two days also being official holidays, though in Chiang Mai the festivities generally spill over into a week-long party. At its core, Songkran marks a new beginning, a time of revitalization, of purification, and of paying respect, as well as an invocation for the monsoon rains to begin. Religious and social rites aside, however, the festival is most spectacularly celebrated in a glorious riot of splashing water that is poured over everyone within range, using everything from buckets, to high-power water pistols and cruising pick-up trucks that hose down all in sight.

It's a fun-packed carnival wherever it is celebrated in the country, but for pageantry, parades, music, dancing and 'Miss Songkran' beauty contests, as well as sheer numbers of celebrants, Chiang Mai is the place to be.

Opposite: Wat Phra Singh, Chiang Mai's largest temple, is important not only architecturally, but also for the venerable Phra Buddha Singh image enshrined here that is an object of devotion.

Above: The picturesque Mae Ya waterfall at Doi Inthanon, Thailand's highest mountain, is a popular day-excursion from Chiang Mai.

Opposite: Wat Phra That Doi Suthep is a glorious sight, resplendent with Lanna-style *chedi*, ornate sanctuaries and intriguing statuary.

HANDICRAFT HIGHWAY

The 12-km (7.5-mile) road from Chiang Mai to the village of San Khamphaeng is lined with shops and factories producing the whole gamut of crafts for which Chiang Mai is famous, affording not only the opportunity to buy but also the chance to see crafts in the making, from silk and other fabrics to silverware, lacquerware, woodcarving and celadon ceramics. The route also takes in the village of Bor Sang, devoted almost entirely to the production of the hand-painted paper umbrellas that are iconic of Chiang Mai.

Among other city temples, Wat Chiang Man is widely regard as the oldest, thought to occupy the site of King Mengrai's camp before the city was constructed. The buildings seen today are of a later date and include a 15th-century *chedi*, a 19th-century wooden *bot*, and two more modern *viharns* that enshrine Buddha statues among which the most important are Phra Setang Khamani, a small ancient crystal figure thought to be endowed with rain-making powers, and Phra Sila, a stone image of Indian origin.

On the edge of town, to the west and northwest respectively, are two very distinct temples, Wat Suan Dork and Wat Chet Yot. The former, 'Flower Garden Temple' as the names translates, is a picturesque site dominated by a bell-shaped *chedi* and intriguing in its complex of small reliquaries containing the ashes of members of Chiang Mai's former royal family. Of contrasting architecture, Wat Chet Yot derives its name from the seven (*chet*) spires of its square *chedi* modelled after the Mahabodhi Temple in Bodh Gaya, India, where the Buddha achieved Enlightenment.

All of Chiang Mai's major temples are rewarding sights, though to see the most glorious you need to venture a few kilometres outside town to the mountain of Doi Suthep. Here, perched near the summit, accessed either by a flight of 290 steps or by funicular railway, is Wat Phra That Doi Suthep, which according to legend was founded in the late 14th century when King Ku Na was seeking a repository for some holy relics. These were placed in a howdah on the back of an elephant which, after being allowed to wander at will, climbed Doi Suthep, stopped near the summit, turned around three times and trumpeted, thus indicating the chosen spot.

The complex seen today dates from the 16th century, though it has been restored a number of times since, and comprises a Lanna-style *chedi* covered with engraved gold plates and two sanctuaries surrounded by cloisters. Lavish and ornate decoration throughout

is matched by magnificent panoramic views of the surrounding countryside and the hills beyond.

With city amenities and small-town charm, Chiang Mai is a place to relax. It's also a base for adventure travel into the hills, with trekking, elephant safaris and mountain biking being among the most popular options. More leisurely day excursions can be made to Lamphun, Doi Inthanon and the Mae Sa valley.

For the history buff, Lamphun, 26 km (16 miles) south of Chiang Mai, is a tranquil little town of great antiquity, founded in the 9th century AD as the capital of the Mon kingdom of Haripunchai. Attesting to this glorious past is Wat Phra That Haripunchai, originally built in 1044 and most prominently featuring a superb 50-m (164-ft) high *chedi* covered in copper plates and topped by a gold umbrella. Also of note is the 14th-century Suwanna Chedi, constructed in the form of a stepped pyramid, and a 19th-century Lanna-style manuscript repository.

Less imposing but of great historical significance is Wat Ku Kut (also known as Wat Chama Devi), distinguished by its two brick *chedis*, which are believed to date from the early 13th century and are rare examples of their kind.

Some 58 km (36 miles) from Chiang Mai, Doi Inthanon National Park makes for a pleasant day out. Encompassing Thailand's highest peak (2565 m/8415 ft), the park covers 700 km² (272 sq miles) and while there is a road to the summit, plenty of hiking trails allow treks into the wild. Magnificent views, waterfalls and excellent opportunities for bird-watching, along with cooler weather compared to that of the Chiang Mai valley, are all part of the attraction.

Although far more developed than Doi Inthanon and with scenery more manicured, the Mae Sa valley, a short drive north of Chiang Mai, is a popular resort area with the atmosphere of a country garden. Adding interest are several orchid farms where visitors can see richly varied and colourful arrays of the nation's most famous flower.

ORCHIDS

So widespread is the orchid in Thailand that it is easy to imagine that it is the national flower. It is not, as it happens, that honour belonging to *Cassia fistula*, or the Golden Shower tree.

However, in its overwhelming profusion, witnessed equally in market stalls overflowing with the blooms, at orchid farms where hybrids are continually produced, or in the more than 1000 wild species that grow in the country's forests, the orchid is an everyday part of Thai life, as well as a valued export item.

Above right: Close to the summit of Doi Inthanon, a *chedi* commemorates the 60th birthday of His Majesty King Bhumibol Adulyadej in 1989.

Opposite above left: In spite of rapidly developing as a modern metropolis, Chiang Mai moves at a slower, more relaxed pace than Bangkok.

Opposite above right: Chiang Mai is renowned for its colourful blooms, annually celebrated in an elaborate flower festival and float parade.

Opposite below: Trekking into the hills on elephant-back is an ideal way for a tourist to take in the scenery with minimal exertion.

Far North

Thailand's far north is associated in the popular mind with the Golden Triangle where, across the borders of three countries, wily opium smugglers lead mule trains along secret jungle trails. Certainly, the borders of Myanmar, Thailand and Laos do meet at a point known at the Golden Triangle, but the drug trade has now been mostly eradicated. That doesn't make the region any less exciting; the mountain scenery is more wild and rugged than that around Chiang Mai, while ancient ruins, hill-tribe villages, river excursions and other eco- and adventure tours are all on the menu.

Chiang Rai, capital of the country's northernmost province, is not obviously the main attraction. It lacks imposing monuments and serves primarily as a comfortable base for exploring the surrounding countryside.

In spite of being founded in 1262, thus pre-dating Chiang Mai by 34 years, Chiang Rai does not flaunt its past. Characterized by unprepossessing rows of concrete shophouses and preserving few monuments to its ancient history, it appears superficially uninspiring. However, as Chiang Mai becomes increasingly a commercial centre, Chiang Rai is by comparison noticeably more traditional and more placid.

Though none are architectural gems, Chiang Rai's handful of old temples are worth more than just a cursory glance. Wat Phra Kaeo has a late Lanna-style chapel and a few distinguished bronze Buddha images. It is, however, best known for its *chedi* where, it is said, Thailand's famous statue of the Emerald Buddha (now enshrined at Bangkok's Wat Phra Kaeo) was first discovered in 1436. Wat Phra Singh is also renowned for an important image, that of Phra Buddha Si Hing, though the original statue has been removed to the temple of same name at Chiang Mai and a copy resides in its place.

Of particular historical note is Wat Ngam Muang. Perched atop a low hill and reached by a short flight of *naga*-flanked steps, it possesses an ancient brick *chedi* which is the reliquary for the remains of King Mengrai.

Wat Doi Tung, located on a hill in the northwest corner of town, again has associations with Mengrai. Tradition has it that this was the vantage point from where he first surveyed the site of what was to become Chiang Rai. Even now it still offers a pleasing prospect of the Kok River that flows by the edge of town.

While Chiang Rai holds more places of interest than a first glance would suggest, it is the countryside beyond which is the area's main attraction. Directly north of the town, the first sights are the two high forested hills of Doi Mae Salong and Doi Tung. Both peaks are accessible by paved roads and offer excellent views of the countryside, while Akha hill-tribe villages add further interest to the landscape.

Doi Mae Salong is the more rugged of the two mountains and is topped by a Kuomintang Chinese village, where it is well worth browsing around the market which sells a bizarre selection of goods ranging from hill-tribe handicrafts to pickled snakes and other traditional Chinese medicines.

Above: The attractions of Doi Mae Salong, accessible by road, include mountain scenery, hill-tribe villages and a Kuomintang Chinese village.

Opposite: The Rai Mae Fah Luang Art and Cultural Park in Chiang Rai is a splendid showcase of traditional Lanna architecture and crafts.

TEMPLE IN WHITE

As every visitor knows, Thailand is a land of temples, but none is quite like Wat Rong Khun, located a dozen kilometres south of Chiang Rai town. Startling white and adorned with a riot of lace-like tracery, the new chapel at this formerly old and run-down temple is simply unique.

It is the creation of Chalermchai Kositpipat, a native of Chiang Rai province and one of the country's most prominent neo-traditionalist artists. 'I wanted to create something totally unconventional, something never done before,' Chalermchai said in a newspaper interview. 'Instead of the usual colourful tiles and golden spires, I came up with the idea to build a pure white temple … decorated only with reflective glass mosaic chips. It would be like a shining crystal of light, of purity, like the teachings of the Lord Buddha.' Stunningly beautiful, it needs to be seen to be believed.

THE GOLDEN TRIANGLE

Opium has been grown as a cash crop in northern Thailand by hill-tribe peoples since the late 19th century. The area that became known as the Golden Triangle is inaccurately pinpointed today as the junction of the borders of Thailand, Myanmar and Laos, but it was in fact a vast tract of hill country spanning all three counties and producing more than half of the world's opium output. Refined into heroin, opium was turned into 'gold' for the traffickers, but not for the hill-tribe farmers, who remained poor.

Thailand outlawed the cultivation of the opium poppy in 1959, but it continued to flourish into the 1960s after which royally initiated crop substitution schemes and other government efforts succeeded in mostly eradicating opium production in Thailand by assisting hill tribes to grow more lucrative, legitimate produce.

An insight into the dark history of Thailand's drug trade can today be gleaned from the excellent Hall of Opium Museum at the 'Golden Triangle' in Chiang Rai province, pictured below.

Doi Tung, on the other hand, has been extensively developed by a foundation established under the auspices of the late Her Royal Highness the Princess Mother. The mountain slopes and hill-tribe villages thus appear more manicured, although the culture of the area has been well preserved. Topping the mountain is Wat Phra That Doi Tung, the region's most sacred shrine. Its twin *chedis* and other temple buildings are the very picture of an Oriental fairytale, an impression enhanced by the scenic views that the 2000-m (6560-ft) high site commands.

From the foot of Doi Tung and Doi Mae Salong you can head either north to Mae Sai, or northeast to Chiang Saen – the two are linked by a good road and so a circular route is also possible.

The border town of Mae Sai is basically one street lined with souvenir stalls, and its main claim to fame is as Thailand's northernmost settlement. Sights are few, although a hilltop vantage point close to the bridge over the Sai river, which forms the boundary with Myanmar, offers good views.

Better sightseeing opportunities are found at the Mekong riverside town of Chiang Saen. This is the site of an ancient city, witnessed in a handful of ruins, notably the lovely Wat Pa Sak *chedi* on the edge of town, while the modern settlement is a tranquil little place drawing definition from its river frontage.

A few kilometres upstream, reached by a paved road, is the popularly, if inaccurately, named Golden Triangle, where the borders of Thailand, Laos and Myanmar meet at the confluence of the Mekong and Ruak rivers. This famous juncture is best viewed by climbing up the small hill to Wat Phra That Phu Khao. Regrettably, however, the once pretty little scene is now cluttered with hotels, guesthouses and souvenir stalls. A better feel for the region is to be had by taking a longtail boat for an exhilarating, high-speed trip downriver to the small Mekong town of Chiang Kong.

Above left: A mother and child pose for the camera in front of the border crossing into Myanmar at Mae Sai, Thailand's northernmost town.

Opposite above left and above right: Brass neck rings are considered a mark of beauty among the women and young girls of the Padaung tribal minority found in this part of Thailand.

Opposite below: The quintessential northern landscape: fertile valleys supporting rice cultivation in the shadow of forested hills.

City of Three Mists

With low, early morning white cloud blanketing the surrounding hills, denser or more lingering depending on the season, Mae Hong Son has been dubbed *Muang Sam Mok*, 'City of Three Mists'. Buried deep in mountain folds, this tiny provincial capital close to the Myanmar border northwest of Chiang Mai has in recent years become a base for trekking, though otherwise a sense of isolation endures.

That Mae Hong Son should retain an independent air is scarcely surprising. Hemmed in on all sides by forested mountains, it was linked with the outside world only in 1965 when a paved road from Chiang Mai was completed, affording a 369-km (229-mile) rollercoaster drive through the hills.

Before there was paved road access, the town had a reputation as being Thailand's 'Siberia' since here was a convenient spot for posting into oblivion government officials who had blotted their copy books. That is no longer the case but the town continues to hold itself aloof, happily tucked away in a valley that could be a contender for Shangri-La.

A distinct character is also preserved by the human factor. The majority of the townsfolk are Thai Yai or Shan, with Karen, Meo, Lisu and Lahu tribespeople adding an exotic touch of colour, while the architecture of the town's older houses and its handful of Buddhist temples is mainly Burmese in style.

There is not an awful lot to do and that, of course, is the main attraction; just to wander around and soak up the small-town charm. To see the town at its liveliest – the only time it is lively – a visit to the morning market is a must. Here, between 6 and 8 am there is an untypical buzz of activity around stalls loaded with fruit, vegetables, spices, meats, clothes and household goods. Hill-tribe people mix with townsfolk, presenting a kaleidoscope of faces ranging from pretty young girls to wizened old women contentedly puffing away on hand-rolled cheroots.

After jostling in the market, a leisurely time can be had exploring Mae Hong Son's only other physical attractions, a handful of Burmese-style temples, the best being Wat Chong Kam and Wat Chong Klang. Both are picturesquely located beside a small lake and both are built in the typically intricate Burmese style with tottering multi-tiered roofs. Of special interest at Wat Chong Klang is a collection of Burmese wooden dolls, the tallest about 1 m (39 in) high, representing figures from one of the traditional stories about the Buddha's previous lives.

Dominating the western edge of town is Doi Kong Mu, a 424-m (1391-ft) high peak topped by Wat Phra That Doi Kong Mu. The two *chedis* here and the several surrounding statues are fascinating, but the real reward is the magnificent bird's eye view of Mae Hong Son, the fertile valley in which it lies and the high encircling mountains of this isolated location.

Lampang

In spite of ranking as the north's third largest city, Lampang is virtually unknown to the international traveller. The neglect is unjustified in that, aside from several important sights, the town retains a traditional character, holding to old-time urban values, symbolized most obviously by it being the only town in Thailand still to have a few of the horse-drawn carriages that were first introduced from England in the early 20th century.

Settlements in the Wang River valley probably flourished long before Chiang Mai was founded in the late 13th century, and it is generally thought that Lampang dates back to the 7th century and was an offshoot of the Haripunchai kingdom centred on present-day Lamphun. Then known as Kelang Nakorn, the town was linked with four outlying fortified settlements, of which one, Wat Phra That Lampang Luang, still stands.

Located some 15 km (9 miles) outside of modern Lampang, Wat Phra That Lampang Luang, raised on a grassy mound and surrounded by thick walls, looks very much the stronghold it once was. Walking up a short *naga*-flanked staircase and passing through an imposing gateway, you enter a spacious compound where the several buildings are dominated by a 45-m (148-ft) high *chedi*, dating from the mid-15th century. The open-side main *viharn* is an equally fine structure with many notable features, including some lovely murals on wooden panels below the roof eaves, which although now rather faded, are still splendid examples of northern-style classical painting.

Enshrined in a compound adjacent to that of Wat Phra That Lampang Luang is the green jasper image of Prakeo Don Tao. Its origins are steeped in legend and it is widely held to have magical powers, which in part accounts for the fact that Wat Phra That Lampang Luang is a popular site for various annual ceremonies, especially Songkran and Loy Krathong.

The site of Lampang shifted over the centuries and the present settlement offers a different historical perspective to the medieval charm of Wat Phra That Lampang Luang. The imprint left on the town today comes from its importance in the late 19th and early 20th centuries, when it served as the headquarters of northern Thailand's then huge logging industry. An inkling of what the town was then like can be glimpsed along Thanon Talad Gao, Old Market Road, which is still lined with wooden Lanna-style homes and Chinese shophouses.

A cultural, as well as a commercial, legacy from the old logging days is also to be found in Lampang's half dozen or so major temples which, because of the one-time population of loggers and merchants from Burma, display variously Lanna and Burmese architectural styles. The latter, perhaps best seen at Wat Sri Chum, is characterized by multi-tiered roofs, intricately carved eaves and a fondness for coloured glass mosaic. In contrast, pure Lanna style can be seen at Wat Pongsanuk Tai, where the compound of a new monastery totally encompasses an old temple, remarkable for its *chedi* and exceptionally fine wooden *mondop*.

Both Burmese and Lanna forms distinguish Lampang's main temple, Wat Phra Kaeo Don Tao, which, in addition to its architectural interest, gains importance as the temporary abode in the 15th century of the Emerald Buddha image now enshrined in Wat Phra Kaeo in Bangkok.

Finally, some 30 km (19 miles) away is the Thai Elephant Conservation Centre, run by Thailand's Forest Industry Organization. This is one of the finest and best run of the elephant camps in the north. There are daily displays which allow visitors to see the animals' skills in traditional logging techniques, as well as modern experiments involving elephants painting and music making.

TEAK

During the first half of the 20th century, teak extraction was a major industry in the north, centred on the towns of Chiang Mai and Lampang and conducted under licence by the big foreign trading houses based in Bangkok, such as the Borneo Company. With elephants trained in forestry work supplying the muscle, logging was conducted on a sustained-yield basis, which allowed for natural reforestation. Felled timber was hauled to river banks where it was lashed into log rafts and floated down to the sawmills of Bangkok.

The industry was fully nationalized in 1960, effectively ending the days of the 'teak wallahs', who until then had been notable characters among Thailand's expatriate community. Subsequently, due to widespread deforestation, logging was banned in 1989.

Opposite: Mostly dating from the 15th century, Wat Phra That Lampang Luang is as attractive as it is historically important.

Nan

Last of the major northern cities, Nan lies close to the eastern edge of the region. Its origins date back to the 13th century when it was the centre of a small remote principality, and its main attraction today is a number of venerable temples, the most important of which is Wat Phumin, a temple of extraordinary charm and beauty.

The main preaching hall dates from the late 16th century and exhibits an untypical cruciform pattern with steps leading up to exquisitely carved entrance doors on each of the four sides. The stairways of the two entrances that parallel the street are flanked by balustrades in the form of *nagas* with the tail at one doorway and the head at the other.

The interior is as charming as the external architecture and is dominated by a magnificent centrepiece of four Buddha statues facing the four cardinal points. The walls are covered with some fascinating mural paintings that depict the story of Chao Kattana Kumara (one of the Buddha's previous incarnations) and, incidentally in their details, illustrate scenes from provincial life. Later restoration work included the amusing addition of foreign ladies and a steamboat, and overall the murals present a charming socio-historical record.

Also of note is the nearby Wat Chang Kham Vora Viharn, which derives its name from its *chedi*, originally built in 1406, which displays seven elephant buttresses on each side of its base. The main attraction, however, is not the architecture but a superb 15th-century gold statue of the walking Buddha housed behind a glass partition in the monks' residence.

Several other temples are worth visiting, the most impressive being Wat Phra That Chae Haeng, situated a couple of kilometres from the town centre. Occupying an elevated spot, reached by a majestic *naga*-flanked approach, Wat Phra That Chae Haeng is an ancient walled temple and in every respect is a most imposing monument, dominated by a 55-m (180-ft) high *chedi* covered with copper plaques. Equally awe-inspiring is the *viharn*, a marvellous structure of Laotian influence characterized by a three-tiered, five-level roof with carved wooden eaves.

There could be no finer monument to Nan and its long history that Wat Phra That Chae Haeng which, with its sense of nobility, power and assurance, encapsulates the grandeur of the past.

BOAT RACES

Nan is renowned for its annual boat racing festival held in October, one of the largest and the most exciting of all the traditional regattas held by many riverine communities around Thailand to celebrate the end of Buddhist Vassa (a period of retreat and abstinence similar to Christian Lent). At this time the river is high after the rains and the stretch in front of the Governor's residence bursts into life as 40 or more sleek *naga*-prowed longboats, manned by up to 50 oarsmen apiece, vie for the honours. The two-day event attracts a number of teams from the various districts of Nan province and the degree of sporting rivalry is high, with the competitors urged to ever greater efforts by bands of wildly enthusiastic spectators who throng the river banks, cheering, yelling and generally contributing to an electrifying atmosphere.

Above: Buddha images facing the four cardinal points are the centrepiece of the rich interior of Wat Phumin in Nan.

Right: Wat Phumin is atypical in its cruciform design with *naga*-flanked steps leading to both front and rear entrances.

Opposite above: Guardian lions stand at the entrance to the chapel of Wat Phra That Chae Haeng in Nan.

Chapter Six

Traditional Thailand

The Northeast

'The place is remote, the food unpalatable, the women unattractive,

and there's no *sanuk*, fun.' This was how Isan, Thailand's northeast region,

was described to a prospective traveller back in the 1950s.

Much has changed over the last half century, travel perceptions not least.

These days visitors will attest to the beauty of Isan's women and most

gourmets will tell you Isan's fiery food is the most exciting

of Thailand's culinary creations.

Opposite above left: The confluence of the Mekong and Mun Rivers at Khong Chiam
in Ubon Ratchathani province.

Above left: Like a religious theme park, Sala Keo Ku in Nong Khai features a strange collection
of statuary depicting gods, goddesses, saints, devils and demons.

Opposite left: The main sanctuary of the hilltop Khmer temple of Phanom Rung is
suddenly revealed after an approach via a steep stairway.

Left: Wat Phra That Phanom, Nakhon Phanom province, is exceptional for its
graceful square-shaped *chedi* in Laotian style.

Traditional Thailand

"The region is intensely rural … its prehistoric sites and ancient ruins attesting to some of the earliest civilizations…"

Today, that quintessential Thai trait of *sanuk*, the jauntiness of Isan's *morlam* folk music and joyousness of its many unique festivals are contagious. Also, no longer is the region remote as it was in the mid-20thcentury because it now enjoys air, road and rail links as good as anywhere in the country.

That said, change in Isan has been less marked than elsewhere in the country and it is here that you can glimpse a traditional Thailand that is fast vanishing. The region is comparatively poor and underdeveloped, its village-centred, agriculture-based economy blighted by low-yield soil and unpredictable rains, while its most visible exports are housemaids, construction workers and others who satisfy Bangkok's demand for unskilled labour.

Culturally the region is distinguished by strong Laotian influence. The Thais here are ethnically more closely related to the Lao than to any of their other neighbours, and this serves to reinforce the individuality of the northeast.

As always, paradoxes abound in Thailand and Isan is no exception. The region is intensely rural, yet its main cities, major communication hubs supporting burgeoning agro-industries, rank as the country's most populous after Bangkok. More surprising is that far from ever being a backwater, Isan possesses a remarkable historical legacy, its prehistoric sites and ancient ruins attesting to some of the earliest civilizations to flourish in Southeast Asia.

The greatest historical heritage is that of the ancient Khmers, who between the late 9th and late 12th centuries dominated what is now northeast Thailand. Their legacy survives in numerous temple ruins that vie in terms of aesthetic and architectural importance, if not in scale, with their more famous counterparts in Cambodia. These monuments are in the distinctive Khmer architectural form of a *prasat*, commonly a cruciform sanctuary topped by a phallic-like tower known as a *prang* and symbolic of the mythological realm of the gods. Originally serving forms of Hinduism and the Khmer cult of the god-king, the temples were later converted to

Left: Khmer sculpture and most especially carved friezes of gods, animals and mythological scenes complement the architecture of Phnom Rung.

Opposite above left: Turning out reproductions of Ban Chiang pottery with its characteristic swirl designs has become a cottage industry.

Opposite above right: Silk weaving is a handicraft traditional to the northeast, the region's most famous fabric being mutmee tie-dyed silk.

Opposite below: A young boy offers alms to a Buddhist monk in the tranquil riverside town of Chiang Khan, Loei province.

MUTMEE SILK

Traditional to the northeast, one of the country's strongest and oldest centres of silk production, mutmee is generally considered the best of Thailand's famous silks. The high reputation of this hand-woven fabric stems from the quality of the material in which only filaments of uniform size and texture are used, and from the complicated dyeing and weaving processes that produce mutmee's distinctively subtle colours and intricate patterns.

In former times, ladies would wear costumes made from mutmee on all auspicious occasions and at major religious ceremonies. Not so long ago, however, the fashion and the handicraft itself had all but vanished. Fortunately, Her Majesty Queen Sirikit has subsequently stimulated fresh interest in Thailand's most traditional silk.

Largely due to the efforts of SUPPORT (Foundation for the Promotion of Supplementary Occupations and Related Techniques), under the patronage of Her Majesty, mutmee weavers have been motivated to revive their craft which is now sustained by a new vogue for the fabric.

To the casual observer the most remarkable fact about mutmee is its design, or rather designs, since there are many traditional patterns that, as with the skills involved, have been passed down over the years. Inspired by nature, the master weavers of old devised patterns that were evocative of flowers, pine trees and other local flora and fauna. These designs are still followed, along with more recent adaptations.

In order to achieve such delicate patterns, mutmee is tie-dyed so as to produce threads comprising several colours and not just one as is usually the case. This is the strongest distinguishing characteristic of the fabric, although the entire production, from rearing silkworms to the binding and dyeing of the thread, is a painstaking process. Once everything is completed and the actual weaving started, a skilled weaver can produce on average one metre (3 ft) of cloth per day.

In contrast to the complicated production of mutmee silk thread, the hand-looms and other equipment used are simple and basic, little changed over the centuries, and yet the finished fabric is one of exquisite texture and beauty.

Buddhist use.

Khmer temple ruins, like other important Isan sights, are scattered throughout the region, which extends over the semi-arid Khorat Plateau, bordered in the north and east by the Mekong River, which marks the boundary with Laos, and in the south by the Dongrak mountain range that divides Thailand from Cambodia. In all, the region covers roughly one-third of Thailand's land mass, and its very vastness can be daunting for the first-time visitor, especially as it lacks any real central base on which to focus and because of the relatively long distances between points of major interest. Accordingly, taking a circular route around the region offers perhaps the easiest introduction.

Gateway

Nakhon Ratchasima, also known as Khorat, 256 km (160 miles) northeast of Bangkok, serves as the gateway to Isan. This is one of Thailand's largest cities though quite distinct from Bangkok in ambience, typically provincial in spite of its size and bustle as a modern transportation hub and commercial centre. Some 15 km (9 miles) north of Khorat and another 5 km (3 miles) east of the main highway are the Khmer temple ruins of Prasat Phanom Wan.

This small but attractive 1000-year-old sanctuary faces a modern monastic building, but otherwise stands in an isolated walled compound. The main building is in fairly good condition and comprises a vaulted chamber leading to a rectangular-based tower. Characteristic Khmer architectural devices are evident in the false and true windows, and over the north entrance to the sanctuary tower a fine carved lintel remains intact.

Atypically, the temple is still in use and several Buddha images, enshrined long after construction, are found inside the chamber. The sight of these, decorated with gold leaf offerings, along with the sweet smell of incense, add a sense of religious awe and serenity.

Further northwest of the highway lies the prehistoric archaeological site of Ban Prasat. A Bronze Age burial site dated to around 1000 BC, Ban Prasat boasts three open excavation pits, of which the first is an impressive 5 m (16 ft) deep, delving down through successive burial levels with skeletons and the shards of pottery buried alongside left in situ.

Being somewhat off the beaten track, Ban Prasat adds considerable charm to the historical interest with an almost palpable air of bucolic calm that pervades the entire village of wooden houses, haystacks, tiny fields, and lotus ponds. Here, aside from placid cows and strutting chickens, you're likely to encounter polite little kids, keen to practise their newly learned English yet careful not to overstep the line of familiarity.

Above: Old city gates recall the historic past of Nakhon Ratchasima, today a bustling transportation hub and commercial centre.

Right: Wat Sala Loi, Nakhon Ratchasima's 'Temple of the Floating Pavilion' is a fine example of Thai modern religious architecture.

Above: Wat Na Phra That, outside Nakhon Ratchasima, boasts a lovely old scripture repository raised on stilts over a pond as protection from ants.

Above left: Prasat Phanom Wan is one of the smaller ancient Khmer temple ruins in the northeast but despite its size, it has a charm of its own.

Left: The sanctuary of Prasat Phanom Wan still serves as an active shrine, and its inner chamber is adorned with Buddha images.

Opposite: The Thao Suranari Memorial honours Khunying Mo, whose valour saved Nakhon Ratchasima from a Lao attack in 1826.

Phimai

Continuing on north you arrive at Phimai Historical Park, unquestionably the most important of all Khmer sites in northeast Thailand. Dating from the end of the 11th century, the original settlement at Phimai occupied an artificial island on the Mun River. As the surviving ruins make clear, this was no minor Khmer outpost but a significant cultural centre linked to Angkor itself by a 225-km (140-mile) royal road. What is more, Phimai's temple layout of moat and outer enclosure, with the main sanctuary inside, bears a marked resemblance to that of Angkor Wat, which, interestingly, Phimai predates.

The principal sanctuary tower, 28-m (92-ft) high, was painstakingly restored by the Thai Fine Arts Department in the 1960s, each stone block dismantled, numbered and then reassembled. Together with its characteristic accompanying structures, all finely proportioned, this is a magnificent building.

Again typical of Khmer temples, the carved lintels, pediments and pilasters of Phimai are a wonder in themselves. The fine workmanship, displayed particularly in the sense of movement and strength achieved by the fluid lines of gods and animals, is wonderfully offset by the white sandstone that makes the carvings all the more striking.

Ban Chiang

Heading further north you pass through the major towns of Khon Kaen and Udon Thani, good examples of the region's vibrant commercial hubs, but otherwise with little to detain the traveller. A few kilometres east of Udon Thani, however, is the important archaeological site of Ban Chiang, where discoveries in the 1970s yielded evidence of a Bronze Age civilization that is believed to have flourished some 4000 years ago.

Preserved as a UNESCO World Heritage Site, Ban Chiang is not spectacular, its one excavation pit being just that, a pit, and it is the museum that is the real attraction. Displayed are examples of the civilization's unique pottery, distinctively decorated with swirl designs, while excellent captions tell the fascinating story of Ban Chiang and the thrill of the archaeological discovery that shed new light on the prehistory of Isan.

Right: Pottery shards left in situ at the archaeological dig at Ban Chiang, a Bronze Age site dating back some 4000 years.

Opposite above left: Delicate sandstone carvings of superb workmanship on lintels, pediments and pilasters are among the wonders of Phimai.

Opposite above right: The superb proportions of Phimai's principal sanctuary tower were brilliantly resorted stone-by-stone in the 1960s by the Thai Fine Arts Department.

Opposite below: Preserved as a well-maintained Historical Park, Phimai is the most important ancient Khmer site in northeast Thailand.

Nong Khai

The main highway north from Nakhon Ratchasima ends at Nong Khai on the banks of the Mekong River, which forms the border between Thailand and Laos and is spanned by the Thai-Lao Friendship Bridge, opened in 1994.

A small leafy town of considerable character, Nong Khai draws much of its fascination from its riverside location and is the kind of place just to laze around. There are, however, a number of venerable temples, Wat Pho Chai being the most important.

Situated in the southeastern part of town, Wat Pho Chai is renowned for enshrining the province's most revered Buddha image, Luang Pho Phra Sai, a smallish but stunning statue with a head of gold and a bronze body set on an elaborate altar. The image is believed to have come from Laos and modern murals in the temple illustrate the story of its being taken across the Mekong on a raft, capsizing during a storm but miraculously floating ashore.

More of a novelty than any thing else, Sala Keo Ku (also known as Wat Khaek), just outside town, is a religious theme park dotted with weird and wonderful statuary depicting Buddhist and Hindu gods, goddesses, saints, devils and demons, as well as some secular sculptures. The park was established in 1978 by Luang Pu Bunleua Sulilat, an old shaman who believed that all religions should be integrated together and presumably employed unskilled craftsmen

THE MEKONG

The Mekong is Southeast Asia's longest river and the world's 11th longest, with a total course of 4350 km (2700 miles). Its drainage basin covers 795,000 km^2 (307,000 sq miles) – an area larger than France – and every year it pours some 475 billion cubic metres of water into the South China Sea.

Rising high up on the Tibetan Plateau, the Mekong flows through China, past Myanmar, touches the northern tip of Thailand and then enters Laos before reaching Chiang Khan in Isan. From here it forms the Thai-Lao border for a stretch of some 750 km (466 miles) until re-entering Laos and subsequently flowing on through Cambodia to its delta in Vietnam.

In Isan, the river is broad and majestic, and at several points, such as Nakhon Phanom, there are fine prospects of its swift flowing waters set against a backdrop of the humped mountains of Laos.

Above: The majestic Mekong River forms much of Isan's northern and eastern borders, affording panoramic views particularly at Nakhon Phanom.

Opposite: Wat Pho Chai in Nong Khai enshrines a revered Buddha image that according to legend miraculously floated ashore after a storm.

NATIONAL PARKS

The natural scenery of the northeast may not possess such obvious beauty as is found elsewhere in the country, but the region does boast a number of national parks where flora and fauna are protected. Most popular is Khao Yai National Park, located roughly midway between Bangkok and Nakhon Ratchasima and thus spreading into the southwestern corner of Isan. Established in 1962 as Thailand's first national park, it covers 219,000 ha (542,000 acres) and supports a good deal of wildlife – elephants, clouded leopards, gibbons, mouse deer and Malaysian sun bears – though you need luck and patience to spot any of it.

However, a simple drive through the park is rewarding for its excellent views of mountain, forest and grassland scenery. Among other notable parks and wildlife preserves in Isan is Phu Kradung National Park in Loei province, which encompasses an extremely scenic table-top plateau covered largely by evergreen forest and sheltering a variety of wildlife and some rare species of birds.

Magnificent scenery can also be seen at Phu Luang National Park, again in Loei, and at Phu Pan National Park, just south of Nakhon Sakhon, while Phu Pha Thoep National Park in Mukdahan, pictured above, is an area of caves and odd mushroom-like rock formations.

to give his vision graphic reality. If of no great aesthetic merit, the park is nonetheless instructive.

Also well worth browsing around is Nong Khai's riverside Tha Sadej Market, which has some good Thai and Lao textiles tucked between the clothing and household goods.

Excursions west of Nong Khai, to Si Chiang Mai and beyond to Chiang Khan in Loei province, afford excellent river views. The former looks directly across to Vientiane, the Lao capital, while the latter is an attractive, tranquil little town standing at the point where the Mekong joins the Thai-Lao border.

That Phanom

To continue the circular route around Isan, travel east of Nong Khai, following the Mekong as it makes a broad curve to the south, leads to Nakhon Phanom, unremarkable except for its outstanding river views, and beyond to That Phanom, site of the northeast's most revered shrine, Wat Phra That Phanom.

The focal point of the shrine is a 57-m (187-ft) square-shaped Lao-style spire (*that*) which has a curious history. In 1975 this ancient spire collapsed after four days of torrential monsoon rains. Some people realistically blamed the disaster on the weather, but in keeping with a local fondness for legends and portents, many others said it was clearly a warning, voicing an old belief that if the spire should fall, so too would Laos. A few months later Laos did undergo a radical change of government.

The spire, now rebuilt by the Thai Fine Arts Department, is a splendid structure, quite different from the temple spires seen in other parts of the country and, legends aside, exploring the temple compound and the museum stimulates interest in what is a remarkable monument in all respects.

Below That Phanom is Mukdahan, the last of Isan's main riverside towns and arguably the most attractive. Like Nakhon Phanom, the town is typified by its beautiful Mekong scenery, though because of busy cross-river trade with its Lao counterpart, Savannakhet, there is further fascination in Mukdahan's market which is strung out along the river frontage. Browsing here presents an eclectic mix of fresh produce, household goods, Isan textiles and other local handicrafts, as well as an assortment of Lao, Chinese and Vietnamese imports.

Opposite: A motorcycle variant of the tuk tuk taxi passes the elaborate gateway of Wat Okat Si Bua Ban in Nakhon Phanom.

Ubon Ratchathani

At Mukdahan the road turns away from the river and heads south to Ubon Ratchathani. Attractively sited on the banks of the Mun River, the town was founded by Lao immigrants in the late 18th century and as such is, to my mind, the most characterful of Isan's big cities, preserving in many ways the traditions and culture of the region. This is most emphatically seen at the colourful annual Candle Festival, when, at the beginning of Buddhist Rains Retreat, huge carved candles are taken in procession to city temples where they will burn throughout the Vassa period of abstinence.

Apart from Ubon Ratchathani National Museum, which offers a good introduction to the history, art and traditional culture of the province from prehistory to modern times, city sights include several interesting temples. The best of these is undoubtedly Wat Thung Si Muang, built in the reign of King Rama III (ruled 1824–51) and intriguing for its beautiful local-style ordination hall, teakwood scripture repository set in the middle of a pond, and old mural paintings.

Also noteworthy are Wat Chaeng, which boasts one of the oldest ordination halls in the province and is a fine, well-preserved example of northeastern-style religious architecture, and the riverside Wat Supattanaram, built in 1853 and remarkable for its ordination hall which blends Thai, Chinese and European architectural forms. On the outskirts of town, Wat Phra That Nong Bua is striking as an almost exact copy of the famous Mahabodhi *stupa* in Bodhgaya, India.

Ubon Ratchathani's picturesque setting is fully revealed on excursions east of the city along the Mun River, where cataracts, the best being Kaeng Saphu, and scenic picnic spots attract families on weekend outings. The journey eastwards ends some 85 km (53 miles) from town at Khong Chiam, where the blue water of the Mun River flows into the muddy brown Mekong, giving rise to the local name *Maenam Song Si*, 'Two Colour River'.

Overall, this is a topographically fascinating area highlighted by, aside from the confluence of the rivers, Sao Chaliang and Pha Taem National Park. The former comprises a curious natural formation of mushroom-shaped rocks that are embedded with fossilized sea shells, pebbles and sand grains, giving rise to the geological deduction that the area must have been on the seabed about a million years ago.

Nearby, Pha Taem National Park covers an area of 140 km² (54 sq miles) and comprises plateaux and hills, though the main attraction is a sheer cliff overlooking the Mekong. Crudely etched on the rock face is a series of prehistoric rock paintings of elephants and fish, as well as hand prints. Of evocative rather than aesthetic value, the paintings have been dated to between 1000 and 3000 years ago, but nothing is known of their creators who were possibly related to the early inhabitants of Ban Chiang.

ROCKETS FOR RAIN

Of all the many festivals special to the northeast, none is as exciting as *Boon Bang Fai*, the Rocket Festival. Held in May as an entreaty to the sky god for plentiful rains, the festival is celebrated in various locations, most famously at Yasothon, northwest of Ubon Ratchathani.

The two-day event is steeped in lore and legend and is marked by a carnival atmosphere and much ribald revelry. The focus of attention, however, is on the huge homemade rockets that are fired to placate the sky god. They are basically bamboo tubes packed with gunpowder, and the successful ones take off with a roar like a jet plane and soar to a considerable height. It is a thrilling display of rocketry as the art must have appeared when it was first invented by the Chinese.

Opposite: The modern Wat Phra That Nong Bua in Ubon Ratchathani was built in 1957 to commemorate the 2500th anniversary of the death of the Lord Buddha. The rectangular *chedi* is an imitation of an Indian style.

Completing the Circle

Heading west from Ubon Ratchathani takes you back to Nakhon Ratchasima, a journey of just under 400 km (250 miles), thus completing your circular swing around Isan, though not before taking in three important ancient Khmer sites.

The first of these, the cliff-top Khmer temple Khao Phra Viharn, lies due south of Ubon Ratchathani in Surin province and spans the Thai-Cambodian border. Indeed, it is a controversial location; international arbitration in 1962 adjudged the temple ruins as belonging to Cambodia, but border disputes still erupt from time to time, effectively closing off the site to visitors even though it is more readily accessible from the Thai side of the frontier.

Built between the late 9th and mid-12th centuries, Khao Phra Viharn is stunningly sited atop a 525-m (1722-ft) overhanging cliff that commands dramatic views of the Cambodian plains. It's an energetic climb but thoroughly rewarding for both the panorama and the exquisite architecture and decorative detail of the temple complex, linear in design and extending for some 850 m (2800 ft) over four levels connected by stairways.

More easily reached are the Khmer ruins of Phanom Rung and Prasat Hin Muang Tam in neighbouring Buriram province. Built between the 10th and 13th centuries, with major construction dating from the 12th century, Phanom Rung was restored and developed as an historical park in the 1980s. Its size is not great compared to that of its Angkor counterparts, but its hilltop location overlooking the Khorat Plateau and the Dongrak mountains is magnificent. The main sanctuary is hidden by its elevation as you enter from the east, and only after climbing a stairway and proceeding along an imposing processional walkway crossed by two *naga* bridges do you suddenly see it, its scale triumphantly enhanced by the height of the approach.

Above: The ancient Khmer ruin of Phanom Rung is made even more imposing by the steep stairway that leads up to the main sanctuary.

Opposite: Recently completed restoration work at Prasat Hin Muang Tam has greatly enhanced appreciation of this 10th-century Khmer sanctuary.

SURIN ROUND-UP

Surin province has traditionally been the home of Thailand's most skilful elephant hunters and trainers, and although the heyday of the elephant's role are now past, a glimpse of the once working relationship between man and beast can be seen at the annual Surin Elephant Round-Up held in November.

Not actually a round-up, it is nonetheless a spectacular extravaganza in which some 100 local elephants are mustered to give displays of how they are captured and trained in the skills used in work, battle and ceremonial.

The event is organized by the Tourism Authority of Thailand, but it is not as kitsch as that might sound and the exciting performance pays genuine tribute to the elephant's exalted status in Thai culture.

The squared-based sanctuary tower, with entrances and antechambers at the four cardinal points, is an imposing monument, although once your eyes have become accustomed to the architecture, one's attention is drawn to the mass of decorative detail. Pediments, lintels of interior and exterior doorways and friezes on walls and pillars are all intricately carved with gods, animals and mythological scenes. And one has a modern story attached to it. The lintel showing the Reclining Vishnu on the antechamber just beyond the eastern portico was airlifted out by thieves with a helicopter in the 1960s and resurfaced in 1973 at the Art Institute of Chicago, from where, after 15 years of wrangling by Thailand's Fine Arts Department, it was finally returned to its rightful resting place.

From Phanom Rung it's a short drive to the base of the hill and Prasat Hin Muang Tam. Dating from the 10th century, the site was until recently in a bad state of decay, with extensive land subsidence giving the impression of a surreal Daliesque picture of melting stone. Now newly restored, with columns and doorways straightened and re-aligned, the ruins have lost something of their former romantic appeal, although the restoration has made the architectural symbolism easier to appreciate.

Much smaller than Phanom Rung, Muang Tam comprises outer and inner enclosures, with a main *prang* surrounded by four smaller towers at the centre of a walled compound. Demarcating the four corners separating the enclosures are L-shaped ceremonial ponds. The site is also rich in carved stonework.

With such a wealth of history, unique traditions and, not least, the simple, unaffected hospitality of the northeasterners, Isan may be somewhat marginalized by Thailand's modern development, but its worth is in no way diminished.

Index

Page numbers in **bold** represent images.